W9-AJP-920

a
National
Historical
Society
book

the Concise
ILLUSTRATED HISTORY of

Stackpole
Books

the CIVIL WAR

Text by **JAMES I. ROBERTSON**

Art selected by **FREDERIC RAY**

THE CONCISE ILLUSTRATED HISTORY OF THE CIVIL WAR

Copyright © 1971 by
The National Historical Society
Published by
STACKPOLE BOOKS
Cameron and Kelker Streets
Harrisburg, Pa. 17105

ISBN O-8117-0423-8
Library of Congress Catalog
Card Number 75-162442

Printed in U.S.A.

*Illustrations are identified as to sources by the
following: (B & L), "Battles & Leaders of the
Civil War"; (LC), Library of Congress; (HW),
"Harper's Weekly"; (FL), "Frank Leslie's"; (SCW),
"The Soldier in Our Civil War"; (NA), The National
Archives; (KA), Kean Archives.*

Contents

1864 in the East — 74

U. S. Grant, made Commander in Chief of Union armies after his brilliant victory at Chattanooga, comes east and takes personal command of the Army of the Potomac. In May he moves across the Rappahannock River toward Richmond, but is halted by Lee in The Wilderness in some of the bloodiest fighting of the war. Instead of retreating, however, Grant moves around Lee and they fight again at Spotsylvania Courthouse, the North Anna River, and finally at Cold Harbor, where Lee wins his final victory of the war. Although Grant loses more than 50,000 men in a few weeks and has to abandon his direct drive on Richmond, he gains an advantage by shifting his army across the James River and nearly seizing the vital rail junction at Petersburg. Lee's forces save Petersburg, but now they are pinned within their fortifications protecting that city and the Confederate capital at Richmond. Lee tries to take off the pressure by sending a small force under Early into Maryland—a force that just misses capturing Washington. Later, Grant sends Sheridan into the Shenandoah Valley, where he destroys Early's little army and ends the threat of Confederate raids across the Potomac. The year closes in the East with Lee's underfed, dwindling army manning its fortifications against Grant's growing force.

1864 in the West — 88

Coinciding with Grant's push in the East, Sherman—now in command of the western armies—undertakes the capture of the key city of Atlanta. His opponent is the skillful Joseph E. Johnston, who balks Sherman at point after point, only to be maneuvered out of his positions by the larger Federal army. Finally Johnston takes refuge in the well-prepared defenses of Atlanta when he is replaced by the rash Hood, who wastes his manpower in a series of foolhardy attacks on the Federals. At last, Hood is forced to abandon Atlanta. This victory, occurring at the time of Sheridan's victories in the Shenandoah, offsets Northern war weariness and aids the re-election of Abraham Lincoln. Hood undertakes a futile excursion into Tennessee, hoping to force Sherman to fall back to protect his communications; instead, Sherman begins his "March to the Sea," laying waste a wide swath of Georgia on his way to Savannah, which he captures on December 22. Hood suffers an overwhelming defeat at the hands of Thomas outside Nashville.

1865 in the East — 97

Time is running out fast for the Confederates. As early as 1863, the Federal army has been recruiting Negroes as soldiers and they have been giving valuable service. The South finally begins recruiting slaves to supplement its exhausted white manpower, but it is too late. A Federal victory at Five Forks leaves Lee no alternative but to abandon Richmond and Petersburg and attempt to join Johnston, now back in command of a small army to the south. He is cut off and surrounded at Appomattox Courthouse, where he surrenders on April 9, 1865, under generous terms, allowing the Rebels to keep their horses and to return to their homes rather than to prisoner-of-war camps.

1865 in the West — 103

Sherman catches his breath in Savannah, then crosses into South Carolina, tearing the countryside apart. His old opponent, Johnston, is unable to stop him although he gains a momentary advantage in the Battle of Bentonville, North Carolina. Learning of Lee's surrender, Johnston himself capitulates to Sherman at Durham Station, in mid-April. The war is over except for minor hostilities in the Deep South and the Trans-Mississippi. By early summer all Confederate soldiers have either surrendered or disbanded.

The War on the Sea — 106

Technical innovations distinguished the naval forces of both North and South. The North's *Monitor* was a revolutionary vessel, possessing high maneuverability and a revolving gun turret. The Confederacy devised water mines, "torpedo boats," and history's first tactical submarine, the *H.L. Hunley*. The South reaped glory at sea from the exploits of its blockade-runners and privateers, notably the *Alabama*, captained by Raphael Semmes, and the *Florida*, commanded by Captain John Newland Maffitt. Preponderance of naval power, however, lay with the North, which used it well to impose a blockade and capture Southern ports. Of crucial importance were the river squadrons, which helped Grant capture Forts Henry and Donelson and gain control of the Mississippi River.

The Heritage of a Civil War — 121

In spite of the staggering costs of the Civil War, more casualties than America suffered in World Wars I and II combined, more than $15 billion in property destroyed, a ruined South, military occupation, years of political corruption, and intolerance, the nation bound up the wounds of conflict to form a more perfect Union, and Americans of African ancestry emerged from slavery.

The War Begins

The Civil War was the most traumatic experience in the life of the United States. Neither North nor South in 1861 could have envisioned the scope, or the horror, of that conflict. Some 3,000,000 men served in the armies; more than 2,200 engagements, ranging from Vermont to the Arizona Territory, occurred; an average of 430 soldiers died each day of the four-year holocaust. In the end, almost as many Americans had perished as in all of the nation's other wars combined.

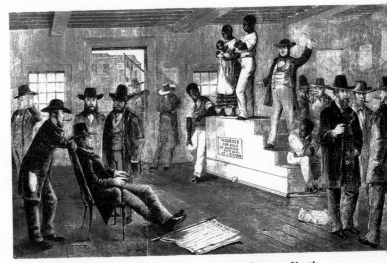

Slavery was basically the cause of the Civil War. To most Northerners, the evil was callously compounded in the slave auction, where men and women were bid for like cattle, and families were broken up as their members were sold to separate buyers.

Cities were ravaged, farms were destroyed, and vast tracts of once-productive soil were laid waste by the indiscriminate appetites of war. Brothers opposed brothers; fathers and sons turned against one another. The continuing progress of the nation was delayed, if not set back, as almost an entire generation evaporated in the flames of battle. From the horror of that conflict emerged a new Union, plus freedom and the promise of equality for Negro slaves. America has never paid so high a price for a definition of its destiny.

Shooting began because men grew tired of shouting. For forty years, Northerners and Southerners argued with increasing vehemence over such issues as slavery, state rights, the conflicting goals of a dynamic, industrializing North and a

The election of Abraham Lincoln in 1860 made him a minority President and gave the "fire-eaters" of the South their excuse for secession. Like most Presidents, and more than most, he grew in stature as a man and a statesman during the four years of war that marked his administration. To the North he came to symbolize the cause for which it fought. (*Alexander Gardner photo from KA*)

Jefferson Davis, first—and only—President of the Confederacy, faced the task of shaping a new nation while waging a defensive war. (*Collections of the Library of Congress*)

static, argricultural South, and the falling from political power of the South that had since colonial days provided the national leadership. By the 1850's compromise, the necessary ingredient to American life, had vanished. Emotion replaced thought; sharp disagreements produced heat; and heat generated fire.

Historians still debate which spark actually produced the explosion. The oldest explanation for the coming of war is the "conspiracy thesis": an Abolitionist Conspiracy in the North, callous to the constitutional designs of the Founding Fathers and interested only in its unrealistic goals, was arrayed against a Slave Power Conspiracy in the South, diabolically resolved to spread slavery throughout the land until it enslaved all peoples, white and black. By the turn of the century, however, such historians as James Ford Rhodes had simplified the cause of the Civil War to a single ingredient: Slavery.

The 20th century has produced a rash of differing interpretations. Charles A. Beard regarded the war as a "second American Revolution" provoked by economic differences between North and South. Many Southern-based historians see the war as a climax to arguments over the supremacy of state rights. Others feel that "Southern nationalism" created a desire to preserve at all costs the South's way of life. Recent writers, such as James G. Randall, take a more psychological approach. To them the war came from the fanaticism of a

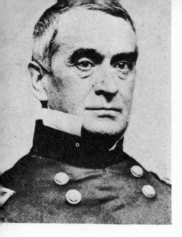

Major (later Brigadier General) Robert Anderson commanded the small force in the hopeless defense of Fort Sumter. Four years later to the day he was present at the fort when the original flag was raised again.

group of hotheads on each side. The great mass of Americans succumbed to radicalism and therefore exhibited the traits of "a blundering generation." Such writers point to modern-day events in America as historical parallels to the coming of the Civil War.

The Civil War began April 12, 1861, with the two-day, bloodless bombardment of Fort Sumter in Charleston Harbor. The dead man in the foreground of this picture from "Harper's Weekly" for April 27 is purely the fancy of the artist.

"Tennessee riflemen entering Winchester from Strasburg, on their way to join the Virginia army." Note the first Confederate flag (which preceded the more famous "Battle Flag") in this picture from July 6, 1861, issue of "Harper's Weekly."

Whatever the cause of war, the 1860 election of Abraham Lincoln as President of the United States shattered the Union. Southerners were unwilling to live under a Republican administration dedicated to antislavery principles. On December 20, 1860, South Carolina officially severed its ties with the Union. In turn, the states of Mississippi, Florida, Alabama, Georgia, Louisiana, and Texas quickly followed suit. A provisional capital was established at Montgomery, Alabama, and the newly elected Confederate President, Jefferson Davis, proclaimed to the world: "All we ask is to be left alone."

Any hope the South had of peaceful secession vanished in the cannon smoke at Fort Sumter. From the beginning the Confederacy insisted that all Federal installations in the South be abandoned. Union authorities refused to consider such demands. Pressures on both sides mounted. When Lincoln announced his intentions to send foodstuffs to a besieged Federal garrison inside uncompleted but strategically located Fort

Sumter, in the harbor of Charleston, South Carolina, Confederates reacted sharply. On April 12, 1861, Southern batteries opened fire. The bloodless bombardment continued for thirty-four hours before Major Robert Anderson surrendered his troops. Lincoln swiftly issued a call for 75,000 troops to "suppress" this "rebellion." The Upper South states of Virginia, Arkansas, Tennessee, and North Carolina, interpreting Lincoln's call as equivalent to a formal declaration of war, left the Union. Secession and war had now become one.

No nation is ever prepared for civil war. This was certainly true of the United States. In 1861, the U.S. Army consisted of but 17,000 men, most of whom were isolated in small pockets along the frontiers of the West. Intensifying this shortage was the fact that hundreds of southern-born officers resigned their commissions to serve with the Confederacy. Nor was the U.S. Navy adequate for its new responsibilities. The American fleet at war's onset numbered only forty-two ships on active service. Eleven of these vessels fell into Confederate hands with the capture of Norfolk, Virginia, in April. The Navy's remaining ships were scattered around the world, carrying out their duty of protecting the nation's citizens, commerce, and interests. In addition, 230 of 1,400 naval officers cast their lot with the Confederacy.

Nevertheless, the North enjoyed overwhelming advantages. The machinery of union had been functioning for over seventy years. The government was established, the currency stable, the bureaucracies experienced. The North consisted of twenty-three states (if we include the border states of Maryland, Kentucky, and Missouri) and 20,700,000 people. The South, in contrast, numbered eleven states and 5,450,000 free citizens, plus 3,654,000 Negro slaves. The North enjoyed a 10 to 1 superiority in manufacturing firms, a 3 to 1 superiority in railroad mileage, a 2 to 1 superiority in manpower, a 30 to 1 superiority in arms production, and incontestable supremacy in finance and commerce. Although the Navy was weak, the North had a veteran merchant marine and large-scale ship-building facilities that could rapidly augment the Navy to the size needed for blockade, amphibious action, and patrol and assault operations on rivers and at sea.

The South seemingly could boast only of superior officers, men more accustomed to outdoor life, the sterling goals of fighting for home and freedom, and a grim determination to maintain announced independence to the last. That European markets were so heavily dependent upon Southern cotton (which, incidentally, provided over 75 percent of the raw material for their textile mills) gave the Southerners a heady sense of power. This factor, however, proved to be a fatal delusion.

The 7th New York parading down Broadway on its way to Washington early in 1861. As this painting by Thomas Nast shows, war enthusiasm then was at its height.

"Filling cartridges at the United States Arsenal at Watertow Massachusetts." Though both sections were unprepared for war, the North had b far the better facilit for production of munitions. (*HW*)

In June 1861 Confederate authorities transferred the Capital from Montgomery, Alabama, to Richmond, Virginia. Both military and political considerations prompted this move. The prestige of Virginia, the richest and most populous of the Southern states, was such as to seem necessary for the success of the Confederacy. Having the Capital nearer the border states, where the heaviest fighting was expected, appeared desirable for a number of reasons. Yet in many respects the transfer was a mistake. Richmond, only 100 miles from Washington, was on the frontier of the Confederacy. It immediately became the primary Federal target; and Virginia consequently became the major battleground for the conflict.

Wartime photograph of the Confederate Capitol, Richmond, Virginia, probably taken in April 1865 after the surrender. Note broken windows. (*NA*)

Cotton bales on the wharves of Charleston Harbor. Cotton was the South's "ace in the hole"; Southerners believed the need for it would bring about European intervention in their favor. (*Courtesy South Carolina Historical Society*)

View of Richmond from Libby Prison. In the foreground
is the canal; at the skyline (left) are tents of Belle Isle prison
camp and (right) the Capitol. (*HW*)

Notes on

1) **The Civil War** was not fought in one arena between
two contending forces. Rather, operations were conducted in
three distinct theaters: the East, extending from the Atlantic
Ocean to the Appalachian Mountains; the West, stretching
from the mountains to the Mississippi River; and the Trans-
Mississippi, a vast undefined region with relatively few people.
Until 1864 and the advent of coordinated efforts by Grant and
Sherman, military affairs in one theater had little bearing or
relationship on army movements elsewhere.

2) Northern armies bore the names of rivers (e. g., Mc-
Clellan's Army of the Potomac), while Southern armies were

This "Balloon View of Washington, D.C." shows the unfinished Capitol dome, the "Long Bridge" across the Potomac, and just to the right of the bridge the incomplete shaft of the Washington Monument. Sketch made from one of "Professor" T. S. C. Lowe's balloons and reproduced in July 27, 1861 "Harper's Weekly."

Military Campaigns

designated by regions (e. g., Lee's Army of Northern Virginia).

3) The North usually referred to a battle by the closest stream, such as Bull Run and Stone's River. In contrast, the South tended to name battles after the nearest community, such as Manassas and Murfreesboro. Quite often, both sides used the same designation for an engagement. Chickamauga, Gettysburg, and The Wilderness are a few examples.

1861 -First Year of the War

Federal thrusts at the perimeters of the Confederacy characterized the first year's fighting. Only one major battle occurred because neither side was prepared for—nor convinced of—the necessity for a major confrontation.

Capitalizing on Union sentiment in the extreme western portions of Virginia, Federal forces moved into that region from Ohio. Small Federal victories at Philippi (June 3), Rich Mountain (July 11), and Carrick's Ford (July 13) against green Confederate troops paved the way for that area ulti-

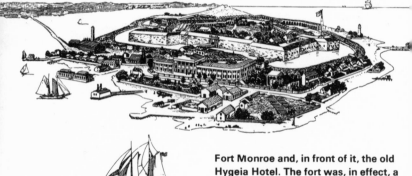

Fort Monroe and, in front of it, the old Hygeia Hotel. The fort was, in effect, a staging area for Union advances on Richmond early in the war. (*B&L*)

mately in 1863 to become the new state of West Virginia. While those Federal troops were enjoying success, another contingent met a sharp reverse. Early in June 1861, a Massachusetts politician-turned-general, Benjamin F. Butler, started from Fort Monroe up the Virginia peninsula toward Richmond. Butler's advance got as far as Big Bethel Church, west of Yorktown where on June 6 a makeshift Confederate force launched an uncoordinated attack that nevertheless had enough velocity to send the Federals in flight back to Hampton Roads.

The loudest and most persistent of Union battle cries during the Civil War was "On to Richmond!" During the four years of conflict, six major Federal offensives were undertaken for the sole purpose of capturing the Confederate (and Virginia) Capital. The first attempt began midway in July 1861. Bowing to demands for action from Washington authorities, Major General Irvin McDowell moved southward across the Potomac River with an army of 35,000 men, mostly three-month

Major General Benjamin F. Butler suffered inglorious defeat in one of the first land battles of the war, at Big Bethel Church, near Yorktown, Virginia.

volunteers. To protect his flank and rear during the advance on Richmond, McDowell had first to seize the vital railroad junction at Manassas. Confederate General P. G. T. Beauregard learned of McDowell's intentions from Washington espionage agent Mrs. Rose Greenhow and others. He quickly

**Major General
Irvin McDowell (*NA*)**

positioned his equally untested 30,000 recruits north of the Junction. On a sultry Sunday, July 21, the Federals assaulted in force by attempting to overwhelm the Confederate left flank. The attacks were initially successful. The Confederate left crumbled in disorder back to the crest of Henry House Hill, where the Virginia brigade of Thomas J. Jackson withstood repeated attacks with the firmness of a stone wall. The arrival of fresh Confederate troops from the Shenandoah Valley turned the tide. The first "rebel yell" echoed across the fields as Southerners drove back McDowell's army in a disorganized retreat. Federal losses were 2,708 men; Confederate, 1,982.

While Southerners basked in the glory of the "great victory" won at First Manassas, and became more convinced that the Yankees could not and would not fight, the North resolutely girded itself for full-scale war. Lincoln named George B. McClellan, 34, as the new army commander and gave him free rein to raise an army of 100,000 or more soldiers. Such a host would be the largest fighting force ever seen in the Western Hemisphere.

Federal probes also occurred in the military theater west of the Appalachian Mountains. On August 10, a blueclad force attacked Confederates at Wilson's Creek, near Springfield, Missouri. The Federals suffered a defeat often termed the "Bull Run of the West." They also lost their commander, the

General Beauregard (*NA*)

Sudley Ford and Church, Bull Run battlefield, scene of McDowell's flanking movement against the Confederate left. (*LC*)

Confederate troops of Bee, Bartow, and Evans rally behind the Robinson house at a crucial point in the Battle of Bull Run. (*B & L*)

promising Nathaniel Lyon, who was killed at the height of the fighting. On November 7, a small Federal army under an unknown general named Ulysses S. Grant managed to hold its own in a collision with Confederates at Belmont, Missouri.

One of the final actions in Virginia during 1861 was a small affair with far-reaching consequences. On October 21, Confederates ambushed a Federal reconnoitering force at Ball's Bluff, a Potomac landmark near Leesburg. The Federals lost over 921 men, including twenty-three officers captured. Numbered among the 234 Federals killed was Oregon Senator Edward D. Baker, commander of the expedition and a close

The rescue of Colonel Baker's body at the Battle of Ball's Bluff.
(*New York Public Library*)

Major General George B. McClellan. Small triumphs in western Virginia brought him over-all command of Union armies in 1862. (*KA*)

friend of Lincoln's. The "Ball's Bluff Disaster" sparked the creation of the Committee on the Conduct of the War, a watchdog Congressional agency that scrutinized closely all Federal military movements thereafter.

Largely overlooked in the big picture of war were inroads made in the South by Union naval forces. The fall of Port Royal, South Carolina on November 7 gave the Federals their first toehold on the South Atlantic coast. Preparations were then undertaken for the seizure of Cape Hatteras, North Carolina, and the eventual recapture of the large naval base at Norfolk, Virginia. And with each month of the war, the Navy strengthened its blockade of the Southern coast.

N.C. Wyeth's mural of the Battle of Wilson's Creek, August 10, 1861. (*Massie— Missouri Resources Div.*)

Joseph E. Johnston. (*LC*)

1862
in the East

It was all so grand and promising, General George B. McClellan thought. For seven months he had developed, drilled, and paraded an army that swelled to 130,000 men. Forced in February by Lincoln to commit the Army of the Potomac to action, McClellan devised an oblique drive on Richmond. He would transfer his huge creation by boat to the Virginia peninsula between the York and James Rivers. Then, as he moved westward up the peninsula toward Richmond,

McDowell's Federal corps would come down from Fredericksburg to lend assistance. Naval forces meanwhile would sweep up the James to guard McClellan's other flank. Joseph E. Johnston's Confederate army, entrenched at Manassas and outnumbered more than two to one, would hardly present serious opposition.

The Peninsular Campaign began with the most famous naval duel of the war—if not of the century. Confederate naval officials had converted the captured Federal warship, *Merrimack*, into an ironclad vessel rechristened the *Virginia*. Packing ten guns and a battering ram, this revolutionary ship early in March gained mementary supremacy in Hampton Roads. Yet the Federals also had been perfecting

Confederate winter quarters at Centreville, Virginia, March 1862. George N. Barnard and James F. Gibson photo. (*LC*)

an ironclad. The *Monitor* resembled "a tin can on a shingle"; and while it lacked the *Virginia's* firepower, it surpassed the Confederate ship in maneuverability.

**The battle that decided the fate of wooden warships.
The *Monitor* and the *Merrimack*, re-christened the *Virginia*.**

On March 9, the two vessels came face to face in Hampton Roads. For three hours each ironclad tried futilely to sink the other. This seemingly inconclusive engagement had three major results: The duel marked the birth of steel navies; had the *Virginia* won, the North would have lost control of the Chesapeake Bay and its many waterways; and the *Monitor's* neutralization of the Confederate ironclad enabled McClellan to put his grand scheme into motion.

Transporting 121,500 soldiers, 14,592 animals, 1,200 wagons and 44 artillery batteries required a flotilla of 389 vessels. By the end of March, McClellan was poised on the Peninsula's tip. So were Johnston and 60,000 Confederates who had hastened to the protection of Richmond. The Federals pushed their way through Yorktown and Williamsburg, then inched through the mud closer to Richmond. On May 31, with Richmond but nine miles away, a desperate Johnston turned and attacked at Seven Pines. Two days of fighting were indecisive, yet the battle had far-reaching consequences. When Johnston fell seriously wounded in the action, General Robert E. Lee succeeded to command of the

McClellan assembles his hosts. Inspection of Union troops at Cumberland Landing on the Pamunkey River, Virginia, May 1862. (*LC*)

Confederate forces. The ever-cautious McClellan ceased his advance to await dry roads and the reinforcements he deemed imperative. He extended his right flank northward for a hopeful link with McDowell's 40,000 men at Fredericksburg. Meanwhile, Confederate batteries at Drewry's Bluff on the James River repulsed a fleet of gunboats seeking to blast its way to Richmond. Federal pressures on the Capital were momentarily contained.

This lithograph shows the wagon trains of the Army of the Potomac en route from the Chickahominy to the James River during the Seven Days' battles. (*LC*)

General Robert E. Lee took command of the Army of Northern Virginia when Johnston was wounded, and went on from a leader to become a legend. (*NA*)

This respite gave Lee time to plan a daring counter-offensive. For the gamble he had in mind, additional troops were needed. He therefore summoned the army of "Stonewall" Jackson, who had just made history in the Shenandoah Valley.

Jackson's movements that spring were not in keeping with the nickname of "Stonewall," bestowed on him at First Manassas, for the stern Calvinist demonstrated that his real genius lay in mobility and surprise. When 1862 began, Jackson was defending the vital Shenandoah Valley. Not only was this area a rich producer of foodstuffs, but it also was a geographical avenue into the heart of the North. Control of the Valley was essential to either side. Hence, as McClellan's Army of the Potomac embarked for the Peninsula, 18,000 Federals under Nathaniel P. Banks moved into the Valley. Jackson's task was twofold and ominous: With but 8,500 soldiers, he had to hold the Valley and prevent Banks from sending aid to McClellan. On March 23, after a forced march, Jackson assailed part of Banks's army south of Winchester at Kernstown. Jackson lost 700 men and was forced to abandon the field, but the ferocity of his attack frightened Washington into holding Banks—and McDowell—as protective buffers for the Northern Capital.

To destroy Jackson and neutralize the Shenandoah, Lincoln then sent three Federal armies into the Valley. More than 63,000 Union soldiers advanced against Jackson from north, west, and east. Jackson obtained 8,000 reinforcements under General Richard S. Ewell—and then struck. Outnumbered as he was, Jackson realized that his only chance was to assail his adversaries separately before they could unite. He therefore left Ewell in Banks's front, marched swiftly up the Valley, turned west at Staunton, and on May 8 routed Robert Milroy's Federal forces at the Battle of McDowell.

The wily "Stonewall" then hastened back down the Valley, used the Massanutten Mountain as a screen, and attempted to get into Banks's rear by coming through the mountain pass at Front Royal. On May 23, Jackson's brigades struck the center

Lieutenant General Thomas J. ("Stonewall") Jackson. (*NA*)

Lieutenant General Richard S. Ewell. (*LC*)

Major General John C. Frémont. (*KA*)

Jackson's "foot cavalry" on the march. (*B&L*)

Union camp at Front Royal, Virginia. From a wartime sketch by Edwin Forbes. (*B&L*)

of Banks's retreating columns at Front Royal. A running fight to and through Winchester followed before Banks retired across the Potomac. Jackson had little time to savor his successes. The lead elements of McDowell's corps were approaching from Fredericksburg; John C. Frémont's army was moving in from the west, and Banks's men recrossed the Potomac.

The Confederates barely escaped being caught in the convergence of those forces. Jackson retreated slowly through Harrisonburg—then turned suddenly. On June 8, Ewell's division inflicted a heavy defeat at Cross Keys on Frémont's forces. The following day, Jackson assaulted James Shields's division of McDowell's corps at Port Republic. By sundown that night, three battered Federal armies were retiring from the Valley.

In forty-eight marching days, Jackson's "foot cavalry" had trudged 676 miles, fought six formal actions and five pitched battles. Although outnumbered by more than three to one, Jackson had been victorious in nearly every engagement. His army inflicted 3,500 casualties, captured another 3,500 Federals, confiscated 10,000 muskets and 9 cannon, cleared the Shenandoah Valley of Federal threats, and so alarmed the Federal Government that the reinforcements McClellan urgently sought were never dispatched. All of this Jackson achieved at a loss of 2,500 men and three guns. Overnight his name became a byword; his fame buoyed the hopes of the South.

Jackson's successful Valley Campaign opened the way for Lee to seize the offensive at Richmond. Lee's cavalry, under the colorful "Jeb" Stuart, made an audacious recon-

Major General J. E. B. ("Jeb") Stuart. His ride around McClellan's army started him on the road to glory as a Confederate cavalry leader. (LC)

naissance in mid-June completely around McClellan's army and confirmed the fact that the Federal right flank was isolated by the rain-swollen Chickahominy River. Lee thereupon decided on his bold gamble: He would shift the bulk of his army from McClellan's front, unite with Jackson, and destroy the Federal army by shattering its exposed wing and taking the enemy in flank.

Confederate charge on Randol's battery at Frayser's Farm. (*B&L*)

What ensued is known as the Seven Days' Campaign. On June 26, Lee's men launched heavy but futile assaults at Mechanicsville against the Federal corps of Fitz John Porter. That night, as McClellan's army began falling back, Jackson's troops arrived from the Valley. Lee attacked Porter again the next day at Gaines's Mill. He broke the Federal line after extremely costly fighting. The Army of the Potomac was now in full retreat to the James River. Lee pressed forward relentlessly in an effort to demolish McClellan's forces. Confederate attacks on the Federal rear, first at Savage Station (June 29) and then at Frayser's Farm (June 30), failed because of Southern commanders' lack of coordination and McClellan's skillful withdrawal tactics. At Malvern Hill on July 1, Lee hurled his army again at McClellan. Federal artillery broke the Confederate assaults. With Federal gunboats supplying both heavy firepower and a secure line of logistics on the James, McClellan was now safe. The Penin-

Chickahominy Swamp, a night-
mare for McClellan's Union army. (*LC*)

The Battle of Malvern Hill, from the Union position.

sular Campaign was over. Fighting in the Seven Days cost
McClellan 15,849 men. Confederate losses were 20,614—
casualties the South could ill afford.

As McClellan extricated himself from the Peninsula, Lee
turned to face a new menace to his beloved state. Union
forces around Washington had been consolidated into an
army under General John Pope, an untested commander who
had won a few easy victories in the West. Pope started
southward along the Orange & Alexandria Railroad. Lee
detached Jackson to blunt this advance until the Army of
Northern Virginia could get up into position. On August 9,
Jackson's heavier force struck Banks's Federals at Cedar
Mountain and won the field after indecisive fighting.

Lee now displayed daring strategy in his effort to destroy
Pope before McClellan's army could arrive. He divided his
forces by sending Jackson on a sweep northward through

A 4th Michigan veteran of the Peninsular Campaign. (*NA*)

Battle of Cedar Mountain, as seen from the Union lines. (*B&L*)

Major General
John Pope, confused
commander of the
Union Army of
Virginia. (*LC*)

Thoroughfare Gap and around Pope's army. Jackson's men seized and destroyed the main Federal supply base at Manassas on August 26, then moved to a strong position on the old Bull Run battlefield to await Pope. The entire Federal army

Jackson's men pillaging the Union supply depot at Manassas Junction. (*B&L*)

Union forces retreat over the Stone Bridge after Second Bull Run. From drawing by Rufus F. Zogbaum. (B&L)

assailed Jackson unsuccessfully on August 29. The remainder of Lee's army came on the field the following day and delivered a counterstroke that sent a bewildered Pope and his beaten army back to Washington. Lee's September 1 attempt at Chantilly to sever Pope's line of retreat failed but cost the North the life of General Philip Kearny, New Jersey's most distinguished soldier. Pope's losses in this Second Manassas Campaign were 14,462 of 73,000 men engaged. Lee's 55,000 troops suffered 9,474 casualties.

Death of Major General Philip Kearny, September 1, 1862, at Chantilly. (B&L)

Harpers Ferry, captured by Jackson in Lee's first Northern invasion. From a wartime photograph. (*KA*)

A number of motives then prompted Lee to invade the North. Union forces in the East were badly demoralized from recent defeats in Virginia; Lee was anxious to relieve the Old Dominion from the telling pressures of war; the chances seemed good for the Confederacy to secure Maryland to its side; and a successful thrust into the Union might bring to the Confederacy the help and recognition from Europe so necessary for ultimate victory.

Early in September, Lee's columns tramped into Maryland and occupied Frederick. As consternation swept through the North, McClellan and the Army of the Potomac gave slow pursuit. Lee next resorted to a move as daring as it was dangerous. He sent Jackson and 25,000 men to capture Harpers Ferry—which would secure the gateway to the

This lithograph depicts a part of the Battle of South Mountain. (*LC*)

Federal attack near the Dunker Church in the bloody Battle of Antietam, as pictured by Thure de Thulstrup.

Valley—while the remainder of the Army of Northern Virginia proceeded toward Hagerstown. McClellan then became beneficiary of a stroke of good luck: He obtained a copy of Lee's orders outlining the disposition of the Confederate army. Yet the Federal commander still labored under delusions as to the enemy's strength. His pursuit continued at a wary pace.

Harpers Ferry, with 10,000 Federals and 30,000 small arms, fell to Jackson on September 15, the day McClellan's men fought their way through the passes of South Mountain. Lee suddenly found himself at Sharpsburg, with his back to the Potomac River and his numerically inferior army rendered even smaller by the absence of Jackson. McClellan's vacillation on the 16th enabled most of Jackson's force to rejoin Lee. Throughout the following day, McClellan launched

Lieutenant General Ambrose P. Hill. His "Light Division" arrived from Harpers Ferry in time to save Lee's right flank at Antietam. (*LC*)

powerful but disjointed assaults that made Antietam Creek "the bloodiest single day of the war." That Lee was able to repulse the onslaughts was due to skillful and heroic defense and the timely arrival of A. P. Hill's "Light Division," which double-timed seventeen miles from Harpers Ferry and delivered a surprise flank attack on the Federal left. Over 25,000 men fell dead or wounded that day.

Confederate dead of S. D. Lee's batteries at Antietam. Dunker Church in background. (*LC*)

Antietam Creek was in a sense a defeat for both armies. Lee's high hopes of Northern conquest ended at Sharpsburg. Yet McClellan permitted Lee on September 18 to retire unmolested to Virginia, thereby throwing away any fruits of victory. On the other hand, Lincoln exploited the battle by issuing five days afterward the preliminary draft of the Emancipation Proclamation. This bold decree granted freedom on January 1, 1863, to all slaves remaining in seceded territory. The Civil War was thus elevated to something more than the mere preservation of the Union, and the Proclamation rendered even more diplomatically perilous any pro-Confederate involvement by European nations.

"Jeb" Stuart gave a small boost to sagging Confederate morale in October, when he and his cavalry again rode around the Army of the Potomac. Stuart's second foray carried him as far north as Chambersburg, Pennsylvania, and provided Lee with much scouting information. This raid

Plume in hat, "Jeb" Stuart leads his cavalry in a second sweep around McClellan's army, after Antietam.

Lincoln visits McClellan after the Battle of Antietam. (*LC*)

lasted twenty-seven hours, covered eighty miles, and cost Stuart but three men.

Lincoln's patience with McClellan's lack of initiative was exhausted. On November 5, he removed the general from command and appointed a Rhode Islander, Ambrose E. Burnside, as his successor. Burnside gained quick approval of a proposal that the Federal army move secretly and swiftly to Fredericksburg, cross the Rappahannock River on pontoon bridges, and advance in a straight line on Richmond. If all went well, Lee would be outmaneuvered before he could ascertain Federal intentions.

Major General Ambrose E. Burnside, unhappy successor to McClellan and author of the Union tragedy at Fredericksburg. (*B&L*)

All did not go well, however. The Federal vanguard reached Fredericksburg on November 17, only to find no pontoons available. By the time they arrived, Lee's army was solidly entrenched on the heights immediately to the south of the city. The Federal army crossed the Rappahannock on December 11. On the 13th, Burnside hurled his divisions in piecemeal frontal assaults against Lee's position. Wave after wave of bluecoated troops were ripped apart by Confederate artillery and infantry. Federal casualties soared to 12,653 men, while Southern losses were only 5,309. Burnside sobbed in his tent, while Lee remarked that "it is well war is so terrible;" otherwise, "we should grow too fond of it!"

In the spring of 1862, Federal forces were assailing Virginia from almost every approach and were as close as nine miles to Richmond. By year's end, the only Federals within fifty miles of the Southern Capital were prisoners of war and soldiers suffering the frustrations of defeat.

Artist Rufus F. Zogbaum shows here the Union bombardment of Fredericksburg. (*B&L*)

The supreme Confederate commander in the West was Albert Sidney Johnston, a veteran soldier and close friend to Jefferson Davis. Johnston was faced with an impossible task. The Confederate Government was resolved to hold onto every acre of seceded territory. Hence, Johnston's 48,000 men were scattered over a 600-mile front from Cumberland Gap

1862 in the West

Albert Sidney Johnston.

to the Mississippi. Federal authorities soon discerned how thin the Southern line was. On January 19-20, 1862, George H. Thomas routed an undermanned Confederate army at Mill Springs, Kentucky.

A week later a second Federal army of 15,000 men, led by U.S. Grant, started through western Kentucky to attack the center of Johnston's defenses. Grant was about to initiate the "river war" by combining soldiers and gunboats to gain con-

"The Campaign in Tennessee—Bombardment of Fort Henry, Tennessee River, Tenn., by the Mississippi Flotilla, Flag Officer Foote, Feb. 6." By Henry Lovie. (*FL*)

trol of the inland waterways of the South. His goals were the Tennessee and Cumberland Rivers, the keys to Tennessee itself. The Confederates had constructed only a single fort for the defense of each stream.

On February 6, 1862, Federal gunboats blasted Fort Henry into submission while Grant was moving his troops into position. With the lower Tennessee River now under control, Grant turned his attention to Fort Donelson on the Cumberland. Federal tactics there had to be reversed. Confederate batteries repulsed the gunboats and forced Grant's men to

Confederate camp—3d Kentucky Infantry at mess before Corinth, Mississippi, May 11, 1862. (*LC*)

operate on their own. Defective Confederate strategy and animosity between the Southern generals inside the fort were the decisive factors in the collapse of Donelson. When Grant replied to a Confederate overture by offering "no terms except unconditional and immediate surrender," more than 13,000 Southern soldiers on February 16 laid down their arms.

The loss of these forts was a heavy setback to morale. A breach in the Confederate bastion had been made: The whole state of Tennessee, as well as Alabama and Mississippi, were now vulnerable to Federal attack. The New York *Times* commented: "The monster is already clutched and in his death struggle."

Major General George H. Thomas, victor at Mill Springs, Kentucky. (*LC*)

General
Ulysses S. Grant, vict
at Fort Donelson, wa
taken by surprise in t
bloody Battle of Shilo

Grant pushed between the two wings of the Confederate army and forced Johnston to fall back to Corinth, Mississippi. By early April, the Federals were near the Mississippi border. However, the Confederates had been strengthening their forces for a counterattack. It came on April 6 at Shiloh, in southern Tennessee, and resulted in one of the severest battles fought in the West. Over 100,000 men took part in the two-day struggle. Johnston's initial assaults caught Grant's inexperienced troops by surprise. Regiments disintegrated as panic-stricken soldiers fled from the field. Determined Union resistance in an area known thereafter as the "Hornet's Nest" momentarily blunted the Confederate drive. By nightfall, however, and despite Johnston's death from a bullet wound, Southern forces had driven Grant's army back a mile, to the bank of the Tennessee River. Don Carlos Buell's Federal reinforcements arrived after dark, and Grant counterattacked the following morning. Ten more hours of fighting ensued before weary Confederates began a sudden withdrawal to their base at Corinth. Halleck, superseding Grant, occupied the town near the end of May. At Shiloh, Grant lost 13,047 men; Confederate casualties were 10,694, about one fourth of their number engaged.

The Battle of Shiloh. Note the point-blank range of the fighting in this Prang lithograph.

Many Northerners, appalled by Grant's high losses, implored Lincoln to remove him from command. The President replied to the criticisms with the statement: "I can't spare this man—he fights!"

Other Union armies in the West made advances during this same period. On March 7-8, at Pea Ridge (or Elkhorn Tavern), Arkansas, Iowan Samuel R. Curtis' 12,000 Federals withstood an assault by 16,000 Confederates that included 3,500 Indians. Curtis assumed the offensive on the second day and won the field, thereby giving the North permanent control of Missouri and northern Arkansas.

Admiral David G. Farragut's capture of New Orleans rates as one of the decisive actions of the war. (*LC*)

Coordinating with Grant's push through Tennessee, John Pope's Federal army embarked on an amphibious operation to clear the upper Mississippi of Confederate outposts. Gunboats and troopships bearing 12,000 men made up the armada that engaged in a March 3-April 8 campaign against New Madrid, Missouri, and Island Number Ten near the northwestern tip of Tennessee. Pope's forces captured both strongholds, as well as 5,000 prisoners, a number of artillery pieces, and large amounts of ammunition and supplies. Again the North had demonstrated the value of joint military and naval operations.

Indians fought at Pea Ridge.

Brigadier General John H. Morgan, colorful Confederate cavalry raider. (*KA*)

One of the Union's most brilliant successes came late in April. A naval squadron under Virginia-born David G. Farragut blasted its way into the Mississippi and seized New Orleans. Army forces under dour Benjamin F. Butler then clamped the city under such rigid military control that the Confederate Government ultimately branded Butler an outlaw. The capture of this all-important port closed the Mississippi to Southern commerce, deprived the Confederacy of a great deal of manufacturing and manpower capacity, and ranks with Vicksburg and Gettysburg as one of the decisive victories of the war.

Strangely enough, Federal advances in the West came to a close that spring. For a year thereafter, the Confederates generally would either be on the offensive or effectively holding their own against Northern onslaughts. Colonel John Hunt Morgan began this shift in military affairs when he led his "Kentucky Cavaliers" on a July foray through his home state. Morgan won four battles, bagged 1,200 Federals, destroyed immense quantities of military stores, created havoc and con-

Braxton Bragg, an expert organizer and disciplinarian, he never knew what to do with success. (*B&L*)

Major General
William S. Rosecrans.
Victor at luka,
Corinth, and
Stone's River, he
failed at Chickamauga.

fusion behind the Union lines, and returned safely to Tennessee—at a cost of fewer than 100 men. Morgan's cavalry compatriot, General Nathan Bedford Forrest, was also active. On July 13, his Tennessee troopers stormed into Murfreesboro and captured the entire Federal garrison of 1,040 Federals.

The major Confederate offensive in the West that year began in August. Braxton Bragg, now commanding the South's Army of Tennessee, invaded Kentucky with the hope of wrenching that state from the Union. On October 8, the armies of Bragg and Buell collided at Perryville. Leadership was lacking on both sides; neither general committed his whole force to action. Yet the fighting was sanguinary, producing 7,600 casualties. Bragg was forced to abandon Kentucky.

Meanwhile, General William S. Rosecrans in Mississippi

Battle of Stone's River.
Advance of
Colonel M. B. Walker's
Union brigade,
January 2, 1863.
(*B&L*)

gained for the Union such convincing victories at Iuka (September 19) and Corinth (October 3-4) that he was shortly named to succeed Buell as commander of the Army of the Ohio. But Rosecrans' confidence was short-lived. On December 31, he attacked Bragg's forces at Stone's River, near Murfreesboro, Tennessee. The two armies pounded each other unmercifully for three days. Bragg finally left the field, having suffered 11,739 losses. The "victory" cost Rosecrans 12,906 men and left his army so weakened that it did not take the offensive again for six months.

A concerted attempt to seize Vicksburg got underway in November when Grant and General William T. Sherman devised a two-pronged assault on the river fortress. But the destruction of a Federal supply base at Holly Springs, Mississippi on December 20 by Southern cavalry under Earl Van Dorn forced Grant back to Memphis. Sherman then attacked alone (December 28-29) and was easily repulsed at Chickasaw Bayou.

John Hunt Morgan's cavalry in the meantime had slashed again through Kentucky. This "Christmas Raid," which cost Morgan two killed and twenty-four wounded, netted 1,887 prisoners in addition to $2,000,000 worth of Federal property destroyed.

Morgan's men were not as well equipped as this Virginia cavalry trooper.

A new year began with cavalry action. In 1863 the principal figure was Colonel John S. Mosby, the legendary "Gray Ghost," who commanded a band of partisan rangers operating in northern Virginia. Mosby's most spectacular feat that year was a March 8 raid on Fairfax, in which he overwhelmed the Federal garrison and personally roused from bed General Edwin Stoughton. Meanwhile, Federal horsemen were trying vainly to match the daring of their Confederate counterparts. Late in April, General George Stoneman's 10,000 troopers made a dash on Lee's communication lines with Richmond. The ten-day foray accomplished little and it deprived the Army of the Potomac of much-needed reconnaissance at a critical time.

1863
in
the
East

Colonel John S. Mosby, elusive Southern partisan cavalry leader in the East.

In January, General Joseph Hooker succeeded Burnside at the head of the Federal army. Hooker displayed great skill in reconstructing units and restoring morale among men demoralized by repeated setbacks. Soon the Union army was at a strength of 134,000 men. Hooker resolved to use strategy and weight of numbers to destroy Robert E. Lee. His plan called for a large portion of his army under General John Sedgwick to hold Lee in front of Fredericksburg, while Hooker and the main body marched westward and crossed the Rappahannock upriver. Then the two Federal wings would crush the Confederate flanks and ram their way to Richmond.

Lee responded with the greatest gamble of his career. He left General Jubal A. Early's division to confront Sedgwick while he and the rest of the army moved into the Wilderness to meet Hooker's main drive. Lee's shift knocked the confidence out of Hooker. The Federal general ordered his forces on the defensive. Lee now seized the initiative. He further divided his meager forces by sending Jackson's corps on a roundabout march to hit Hooker's unprotected right flank. Late in the

Close fighting at Chancellorsville

Major General Joseph Hooker, successor to Burnside. Brilliant organizer and strategic planner, he lost his nerve at Chancellorsville. (LC)

Major General Winfield S. Hancock and his II Corps division commanders: Barlow, Birney, and Gibbon. (NA)

afternoon of May 2, Jackson's men exploded from the woods and shattered an entire Union corps. Darkness prevented the Confederates from pressing their advantage. Near 9 p.m. that evening, while reconnoitering the Federal lines, Jackson was accidentally shot by his own men. General J.E.B. Stuart assumed temporary command of Jackson's corps.

The next day, Stuart's determined soldiers assailed Hooker

from the west while Lee personally led the remainder of his forces against Hooker from the south. Hooker's wing crumbled and began filing back to the Rappahannock. Lee received word during this action that Early's line had broken in the face of Sedgwick's advance from Fredericksburg. Lee left Stuart to continue pressing Hooker while he took a portion of the Confederate army to stop Sedgwick. During May 4-5, Lee defeated Sedgwick at Salem Church and sent this Federal wing reeling northward. Lee countermarched his weary soldiers to deliver a death blow to Hooker—only to find that the other wing of a force Hooker had termed "the finest army of the planet" had retreated across the Rappahannock.

Chancellorsville was a brilliant success for Lee, but costly to both sides. Hooker lost 17,278 men. Numbered among the 12,821 Southern casualties was the incomparable "Stonewall" Jackson, who died May 10 of complications from his wounds. With Jackson's death, an era in Lee's tactics passed away. The startling flank attacks that brought smashing victory at Second Manassas and Chancellorsville never occurred again.

The decisiveness of the Chancellorsville victory, the need to gain supplies, the fading hope of European recognition, and the possibility of striking a final blow at the Union, persuaded Lee to initiate a second invasion of the North. On June 3 the Confederate army began maneuvering for a move across the Potomac. Six days later, 10,000 Federal cavalry under General Alfred Pleasonton struck a like number of Confederate troopers Stuart had assembled for a review on the previous

Major General George G. Meade won at Gettysburg but was slow to follow up his victory and try to destroy Lee's army. *(LC)*

Major General George E. Pickett is about to lead his famous assault in this painting by H. A. Ogden. *(LC)*

day. For eight hours at Brandy Station the two forces exchanged saber-flourishing cavalry charges. The Confederates gained a hard-earned victory, but the Union cavalry gained a new-found respect.

Lee's army cleared Federals from Winchester on June 14-15 and then used the Shenandoah "avenue" to advance across Maryland and into Pennsylvania. Hooker's timidity in combating this invasion provoked Lincoln into appointing General George G. Meade to lead the Army of the Potomac. Meade, a dedicated soldier from Pennsylvania, had been in command but three days when the vanguards of the two veteran armies collided accidentally at the crossroads town of Gettysburg. "The greatest battle fought in the Western Hemisphere" erupted. For three days, more than 163,000 men waged a vicious, unyielding fight. Lee attacked repeatedly but could not dislodge the Federals from positions extending over a four-mile front.

avalry charge at Brandy Station, Virginia. Though they retired
m this fight, Union cavalry gained self-confidence. Edwin
rbes drawing. *(LC)*

Battle of Gettysburg. Major General Winfield S. Hancock directs the defense at The Angle. Note II Corps flag (left). Painting by Thure de Thulstrup.

The climax of the battle came on the afternoon of July 3, when Confederate General George E. Pickett led a heroic but fruitless charge against the center of the Union lines. Pickett lost 7,000 of 15,000 men. With fields drenched in blood, the battle of Gettysburg then ended. The two armies had suffered more than 51,000 casualties.

Again Lee was allowed to make an orderly retreat toward Virginia. Not until the night of July 13-14 were the Confederates able to ford the rain-swollen Potomac River. Thus Meade's decision to attack the strongly entrenched Confederates on the 14th came too late, and he lost the opportunity of possibly destroying Lee and ending the war in the East. This failure tarnished much of the luster gained from the victory at Gettysburg.

The armies of Lee and Meade spent the remainder of the year jockeying for position in northern Virginia. Lee in October made a feint toward Washington that caused Meade to retire to Centreville. Late in November, Meade assumed the offensive and pushed southward almost to Culpeper. For several days the two armies maneuvered at Mine Run. Lee held an almost impregnable position, and Meade prudently withdrew to the Rapidan River on December 1. This ended active operations in the East for the winter.

Major General
John C. Pemberton
(*B&L*)

1863 in the West

Rear-Admiral Porter's flotilla arriving below Vicksburg on the night of April 16, 1863—in the foreground General W. T. Sherman going to the flag-ship "Benton." (*B&L*)

Highlighting the 1863 actions in the West were Grant's extraordinary operations against the Confederate "Gibraltar of the West," Vicksburg. The campaign began in January, when General John A. McClernand led a Federal amphibious expedition fifty miles up the Arkansas River to capture Fort Hindman at Arkansas Post. An attempt by Sherman's men in January-February to cut a canal across the peninsula opposite Vicksburg failed and convinced Grant to concentrate his forces for an all-out offensive against the city. To soften up the region, Grant that spring sent Colonel Benjamin H. Grierson and 1,700 cavalrymen on a raid Grant later termed "one of the most brilliant exploits of the war." Grierson's men fought their way from La Grange, Tennessee, to Baton Rouge, Louisiana; in the process they killed or wounded 100 Confederate soldiers, captured 500 others, destroyed 60 miles of railroad and 3,000 small arms, and set the torch to tons of Confederate government stores.

Meanwhile, Grant's army crossed the Mississippi at Milliken's Bend and marched southward through Louisiana to a point far below Vicksburg. Admiral David D. Porter's fleet blasted its way downriver past the Vicksburg defenses and joined Grant. With gunboats providing security on the river, Grant's 40,000 troops crossed into Mississippi. The Federal army was cut off from all supply bases; yet in less than three weeks a determined Grant led his forces to victories at Port Gibson, Raymond, Jackson, Champion's Hill, and Big Black River. Having interposed between the Southern forces of Joseph E. Johnston and John C. Pemberton's Vicksburg defenders, Grant invested the town and initiated an ever-tightening siege. Union land and river forces slowly forced Vicksburg into submission. The defenders were reduced to living in caves and eating mules, dogs, and—according to some—rats. On July 4, Pemberton surrendered the city, its 30,000 defenders, 172 cannon, and 60,000 muskets. Five days later, the 6,000-man garrison downriver at Port Hudson struck its colors. "The Father of Waters," a joyful Lincoln exclaimed, "again goes unvexed to the sea!" In addition, the entire Trans-Mississippi had been sundered from the Confederacy.

Lost in the impact of the Vicksburg Campaign was John Hunt Morgan's dramatic but unrewarding "Ohio Raid" later that summer. With 2,500 mounted infantry, Morgan cut a swath through central Kentucky and crossed the Ohio River into southern Indiana, slashed through the suburbs of Cin-

The 4th Minnesota marching into Vicksburg, July 4, 1863. From painting by F. D. Millet. (*Courtesy Minnesota Historical Society*)

Naval bombardment of Port Hudson, last Confederate stronghold on the Mississippi. (*HW*)

Lieutenant General James Longstreet. His men made the difference in the Confederate victory at Chickamauga. (*Cook Coll., Valentine Museum*)

cinnati, and swept eastward until Federals dispersed the raiders. Morgan destroyed $500,000 worth of property before he and most of his band were captured and confined in a Columbus, Ohio prison. Morgan escaped in November but died ten months later when Federal troops surprised him at Greenville, Tennessee.

By September 1863, Rosecrans had maneuvered Bragg from Chattanooga and occupied that strategic city. Bragg, a skillful organizer, now proved himself an inept field commander. On September 19, Bragg's 58,000 men engaged Rosecrans' 54,000 at Chickamauga Station, a few miles southeast of Chattanooga. The Confederate attacks reflected the general's lack of confidence and resourcefulness. General James Longstreet and 11,000 men from Lee's army arrived as reinforcements. In the second day's fighting, Longstreet's veterans drove through a gap in Rosecrans' lines and sent the entire Federal

Grant plans strategy to relieve Confederate siege of Chattanooga. From painting by Thure de Thulstrup.

Confederate line of battle in the tangled woods at Chickamauga. (*B&L*)

right (along with Rosecrans himself) fleeing pell-mell back to Chattanooga. But the Federal left, under General George H. Thomas, refused to break in the face of repeated assaults by superior numbers. Thomas' stand earned him the sobriquet "Rock of Chickamauga," and possibly prevented the destruction of the whole Federal army. Rosecrans suffered 16,170 casualties; Bragg's losses were 18,454 men.

Bragg refused to exploit the victory, barren though it was. Instead, he posted his 40,000 men on the hills overlooking Chattanooga and laid siege to the city. Thomas replaced the stunned Rosecrans as head of the army. Grant, now supreme Federal commander in the West, began funneling reinforcements into Chattanooga via the Tennessee River line. Grant soon had supply lines open and 60,000 soldiers at hand. He then struck back. For three days (November 23-25), and from three directions, Federals hammered at the Southern lines. On November 25, Thomas' Army of the Cumberland scaled Missionary Ridge without orders and carried the heights. A demoralized Confederate army abandoned Chattanooga and retired into Georgia. Securing this remaining part of Tennessee cost Grant 5,824 troops. Bragg lost 6,667 irreplaceable soldiers.

Federal advances in the West during 1863 sounded the death knell of the Confederacy.

In addition to the era-ending campaigns of Vicksburg and Gettysburg, the year 1863 was epochal in another respect: For the first time, America made major use of Negroes as combat soldiers.

The opportunity for blacks to fight—and die—for their freedom did not come easily. Using former slaves as soldiers evolved over painful stepping-stones of hostility, discrimination, and ill will. Early in the war, Federal authorities were willing to employ ex-slaves as laborers in Northern armies. Yet because of the popular belief of whites in the Negro's biological inferiority, the North was extremely reluctant to uniform and arm blacks to fight alongside whites.

Attempts in 1862 to raise Negro regiments in Kansas and the occupied portions of South Carolina and Louisiana were ill-organized and too premature to be successful. In the autumn of that year, however, the Federal Government abandoned its lukewarm attitude toward the use of Negroes as soldiers. The war was then going badly for the Union; more manpower was needed; and Lincoln came to see that if the Emancipation Proclamation was ever to have real and lasting meaning blacks had to be given the chance to assist actively in the war for their liberation.

The War Department moved quickly in 1863 to implement the new policy. Recruitment was systematized, officer procurement regularized, training camps established, and a Bureau for Colored Troops created to administer the whole program. Yet the majority of Negro recruits were initially and justifiably unhappy. Underpaid, assigned mostly to menial tasks, and commanded always by white officers, black soldiers were stymied repeatedly in efforts to demonstrate their military worth. That the use of Negroes as soldiers ultimately succeeded so well is attributable to three factors: the indefatigable labors of Adjutant General Lorenzo Thomas (who personally stimulated 76,000 Negro recruitments and raised fifty regiments); a changing, more positive attitude among high-ranking Union officers toward the use of black soldiers; and— most importantly of all—the performance of Negroes in battle.

Proud Negro soldiers of the Union Army. (*LC*)

Hinks's Negro division bringing in guns captured at Baylor's farm near Petersburg, Va.

While Negro soldiers of the Civil War participated in at least 39 major battles and 410 minor engagements, black troops are remembered principally for several 1863 and 1864 engagements. They demonstrated commendable valor in futile assaults at Port Hudson, Louisiana (May 27, 1863) and Fort Wagner, South Carolina (July 18, 1863), while other, equally untested black troops made a brief and disastrous stand at Milliken's Bend, Louisiana (June 7, 1863).

Southern reactions at the sight of Negroes in blue uniforms had overtones of barbarity in such 1864 engagements as

Olustee, Florida; Fort Pillow, Tennessee; Poison Spring, Arkansas; at Petersburg, Virginia, in the "Battle of the Crater," and at Saltville, Virginia. Yet it was after two days of bitter fighting at Nashville that General George H. Thomas rendered the final verdict: "Gentlemen, the question is settled. Negroes will fight."

Indeed they did. A total of 178,895 Negroes flocked to the colors of 120 infantry regiments, twelve heavy artillery regiments, ten light artillery batteries, and seven cavalry regiments. Their numbers constituted 12 percent of the North's fighting forces. Their death rate was unusually high: 68,178 men, of whom 2,751 were killed in action. Most of the remainder were victims of disease. Fourteen black soldiers re-

ceived the Medal of Honor. Color Sergeant Anselmas Planciancois of the 1st Louisiana Native Guards was not among
that number. Yet on the morning before the assault on Port
Hudson, Planciancois received the regimental flag with the
vow: "Colonel, I will bring back the colors with honor or
report to God the reason why." Mortally wounded in the
action that followed, the sergeant's final act was to hug the
flag to his breast.

**Assault of the 2d Louisiana (Colored) Regiment on the
Confederate works at Port Hudson, May 27, 1863. Negroes
proved their valor here and elsewhere. From sketch by
Frank B. Schell.**

1864
in the East

The war assumed a more terrible character in 1864. On March 9, General U. S. Grant came east to take command of all Federal armies. Grant's strategy was brutally simple: The North would henceforth wage total war. All Federal forces would plow ahead in an unrelenting drive to apply pressure at all points of the Confederacy. Battle casualties, war weariness, and Federal occupation of large chunks

Grim fighting in The Wilderness.

Rescuing wounded
from the burning woods
of The Wilderness.
Drawing by
A. R. Waud. (*LC*)

The war is over for this
Confederate soldier. (*LC*)

of Southern territory had reduced Confederate arms appreciably. Grant reasoned that the South's depleted armies could not successfully defend every sector. Nor could it recoup losses in the face of seemingly unlimited Northern manpower. A war of attrition, Grant called it; sledgehammer tactics, his critics would charge.

In May, Grant's strategy burst upon Virginia. Three separate offensives began almost simultaneously. Some 6,000 troops under Franz Sigel moved into the Shenandoah Valley; Benjamin F. Butler and 36,000 men in the Army of the James started up the Peninsula from Fort Monroe; and Grant, traveling with the 118,700 Federals in the Army of the Potomac, crossed the Rapidan to interpose himself between Lee's 60,000 Confederates and Richmond.

The main Union drive quickly became entangled in the Wilderness, an area of thick forests and dense undergrowth west of Fredericksburg. On May 5, the hosts of Lee and Grant came to grips in the wooded darkness. Neither cavalry nor

Union assault at Bloody Angle, Spotsylvania. This scene of some of the war's bloodiest fighting was painted by Thure de Thulstrup.

artillery could take any part because of the tangled forests. Infantry were left alone to grope blindly after unseen enemies. Organization disintegrated as the two armies attacked and counterattacked. Flames roaring through the underbrush cremated scores of wounded men. For two days the inferno of battle raged.

On May 7, having suffered 17,666 losses, Grant broke off the conflict and sidestepped to the east in an effort to turn Lee's right. The Army of Northern Virginia had suffered 11,400 casualties in The Wilderness, but it won the race to Spotsylvania Court House and was waiting entrenched when Grant's forces arrived. Eleven days (May 10-21) of intermittent but heavy fighting ensued. The climax of this action came in fourteen hours of battle on May 12, when Federals temporarily overran a sector of Lee's lines now known as the

"Bloody Angle." The Spotsylvania stalemate cost Lee untold casualties and Grant about 18,000. Especially painful to Lee was the death of the dashing "Jeb" Stuart, mortally wounded on May 11 in a cavalry fight at Yellow Tavern.

Grant continued his southeastward movements. "I propose to fight it out on this line," he vowed, "if it takes all summer." Early in June his army reached Cold Harbor, a strategic crossroads not far from Richmond. But again Lee's men blocked the advance. Grant lost his patience and ordered three corps to make direct frontal attacks on the strong Confederate

Pontoon bridge at Benham's Wharf, Belle Plain, Virginia. (NA)

works. The result was the June 3 battle of Cold Harbor, which many consider a massacre. Federal troops made no fewer than fourteen assaults on Lee's lines. Not one succeeded. In the opening stages of the conflict, over 7,200 Federals fell dead or maimed in a half hour's action. A broiling sun intensified the suffering of the wounded, hundreds of whom lay unattended on the field for more than a day.

In less than a month, the Army of the Potomac was reeling from 55,000 losses—close to the strength of Lee's army at the outset of the campaign. Yet Grant was unswayed. Knowing that Lee had incurred proportionately higher casualties than the North seemed to Grant to make the sacrifices worthwhile. After Cold Harbor, however, Grant altered his strategy. He secretly began shifting his army across the James on the night of June 12. Columns of men filed across a pontoon bridge more than 2,500 feet long and headed for Petersburg, a vital rail junction twenty-five miles south of Richmond. Seizing Petersburg and its railroads would force Lee to come out of his works and meet the Federal army in open combat.

The Federal transfer caught Lee by surprise and almost outflanked the Confederate army from Richmond. Grant's new movement might easily have succeeded had Butler's Army of the James not fallen victim to its commander's ineptitude. Butler had started westward from Fort Monroe as Grant had thrust into The Wilderness. Yet the slowness of Butler's advance enabled General P. G. T. Beauregard at Petersburg to assemble hastily an "army" of 3,500 soldiers, militia, and shopkeepers. The appearance of this heterogeneous force so unnerved Butler that he withdrew his army to Bermuda Hundred and a thin stretch of land lying between the James and Appomattox Rivers. Beauregard promptly entrenched his men across the narrow opening to that peninsula. Grant observed disgustedly that Butler's force was "as completely shut off from further operations . . . as if it had been in a bottle strongly corked."

Beauregard pulled back at Grant's approach. The Southern general's indomitable defense of Petersburg during four days of attack (June 15-18) by the lead elements of Grant's army saved the city—and probably prolonged the war—while inflicting several thousand casualties on the Federal army. The arrival of Lee and the Army of Northern Virginia convinced Grant to switch to the siege operations that proved so successful at Vicksburg. Federal troops began constructing an elaborate network of trenches and earthworks on the eastern front of Petersburg.

Grant (booted, on bench) writes orders during a halt with his staff at Bethesda Church in The Wilderness Campaign. (*LC*)

Lee countered desperately by trying to divert Grant's attention to the Shenandoah Valley, where things had not gone well for the Union.

Franz Sigel's advance into that region in May got only as far as New Market. Confederate General John C. Breckinridge put together a hodgepodge force of 4,500, including a contingent of cadets from the Virginia Military Institute, and moved down the Valley to confront Sigel. On the afternoon of May 15, the outnumbered Confederates launched a heavy assault. Southern losses mounted swiftly and forced Breckinridge to call on the VMI cadets in reserve. The 247 youths

Major General John C. Breckinridge routed Sigel's Union force at New Market, Virginia. (*Cook Coll., Valentine Museum*)

Fort Sedgwick (Fort Hell) at Petersburg, a Union strongpoint. (*NA*)

made a bold charge across the rain-swept field and helped break Sigel's line, precipitating a rout of the Federal army. Sigel lost 831 men. Listed among the 577 Confederates casualties were ten VMI cadets killed and forty-seven wounded.

Grant replaced Sigel with stern David Hunter, who wasted no time in stabbing again at the Valley. On June 6, Hunter struck a skeleton army of Confederates at Piedmont, south of Harrisonburg. Federals overwhelmed the small force, killed its commander, General William E. "Grumble" Jones, and seized 1,000 prisoners. Hunter burned his way to Lexington, then cut eastward across the mountains to Lynchburg.

Lee had just won his last victory—Cold Harbor—when this occurred. He detached General Jubal A. Early and Jackson's old corps to block Hunter. Early's men rushed to Lynchburg and nipped at Hunter's heels as the Federals fled to West Virginia. The Valley was momentarily clear of Federal invaders. With Lee anxious to break Grant's hold in front of

Petersburg, Early then started down the Valley and into Maryland to threaten Washington from the north. The Confederates were so delayed by a battle at Monocacy, Maryland on July 9 that by the time Early reached the outskirts of the Northern Capital, reinforcements from Grant's army were manning the city's defenses. While Early demonstrated briefly against the works, Lincoln rode to the front and watched part of the action from atop a Federal parapet—thus becoming the only President ever to come under enemy fire. Early soon concluded that the Washington defenses were too strong for his meager forces. His Confederates withdrew to Virginia in disappointment.

Grant now ordered Hunter to move back into the Valley "to eat out Virginia clear and clean as far as they go, so that crows flying over it for the balance of the season will have to carry their provender with them."

Charge of the VMI cadets at New Market. Painted by Benjamin West Clinedinst.

Major General Jubal A. Early almost captured Washington, D.C. (*LC*)

Bantam-sized Major General Philip H. Sheridan finally won control of the Shenandoah Valley. (*NA*)

Hunter's hesitancy in tangling again with Early caused Grant to replace him with General Philip H. Sheridan. This pint-sized cavalryman promptly mustered 40,000 men and moved directly on Early's 12,000 troops at Winchester. Sheridan struck the Confederates first at Opequon Creek (September 19) and then at Fisher's Hill (September 22). Early lost almost 5,000 men in the two bitterly fought engagements. The Southerners retreated up the Valley with Sheridan's army—dented by 3,200 casualties—in slow pursuit.

The Federal army encamped at Cedar Creek, near Strasburg, while Sheridan journeyed to Washington for a military conference. Early received enough reinforcements from Lee to bring his army back to 12,000 men. On October 19 the Confederates delivered a surprise attack at Cedar Creek that sent the major portion of the Federals fleeing in panic from the field. But Sheridan made a now-famous ride from Winchester, rallied his broken columns, and hurled a full-scale counterassault that routed Early's meager forces. Early lost 2,910 men, 25 cannon, all of his ammunition wagons, and most of his baggage and forage wagons.

Fort Brady, on the James River, was similar to the forts ringing Washington. (*LC*)

Sheridan now controlled the Shenandoah. His men completed a systematic devastation of the area; the "breadbasket of the Confederacy" was reduced to crumbs.

At Petersburg, meanwhile, Grant had completely immobilized Lee's dwindling army. Both Lee and Grant realized that if the Confederates left their trenches, Petersburg and Richmond would quickly fall. Lee therefore had no alternative but to maintain his position.

Sheridan rides from Winchester to
rally his troops retreating from
Cedar Creek. Drawing by A. R. Waud. (*LC*)

Sheridan inde.

Grant was not idle during this time. He steadily advanced his siege lines to the southwest, a move that threatened the last two railroads leading to Richmond and, at the same time, stretched Lee's already thin defenses ever farther. In addition, Grant made periodic stabs at the Confederate lines in attempts at a breakthrough.

Early surprises the VIII Corps
of Sheridan's army at
Cedar Creek, Virginia.

The exploding of the mine at Petersburg.

Mahone's Confederate division counterattacks in the fighting at The Crater. The Union assault failed because of inept leadership.

The most famous of these attacks was the July 30 "Battle of the Crater." Coal miners in the 48th Pennsylvania Infantry volunteered to dig a tunnel to a point beneath the Confederate works southeast of Petersburg. A large charge of explosives would be detonated at the end of the shaft. In the ensuing smoke, confusion, and death, heavy Federal columns would drive through the breach and widen the gap in Lee's lines. Grant saw distinct possibilities in the extraordinary proposal and granted approval.

The tunnel, when completed, stretched 511 feet from the Federal lines to beneath a Confederate artillery emplacement. Early on the morning of July 30 about 8,000 pounds of gunpowder exploded and blasted a hole 170 feet long, over 60 feet wide, and 30 feet deep. Federal troops easily occupied the area around the crater, but the important second wave of Federals broke down from incompetent leadership and lack of aggressiveness. Confederates recaptured the sector late in the afternoon after some of the most vicious fighting of the war. The episode, which Grant characterized as a "stupendous failure," cost 4,000 Federal casualties. Confederate losses were about 1,200, including 278 men killed in the blast.

Grant returned to more orthodox siege tactics. With naval

vessels running supplies regularly up the James to the main supply base at City Point (now Hopewell), Grant's forces became increasingly stronger. Time was now on the Union side; and as the siege continued month after month, hunger and exposure took a heavy toll of Lee's dwindling army.

City Point, Virginia. This supply depot funnelled food, munitions, and other war essentials, to Grant's besieging army at Petersburg. (*NA*)

1864 in

Observers **invariably commented on the "half-wild expression" of his eyes,** his "terrible cerebral excitement," his incessant smoking, and complete disregard for food and sleep. Many war correspondents considered him dangerously mad. Most of the Confederacy came to that opinion in 1864, when General William Tecumseh Sherman made his name anathema in the South.

With Grant's promotion to General in Chief, Sherman became supreme commander of the Federal armies in the West. "Cump" Sherman was a man who wasted neither thought nor time. He regarded the Confederacy as an arch enemy that

Major General William T. Sherman. He waged "total war" in his Atlanta Campaign, his March to the Sea, and his sweep through the Carolinas. (*LC*)

he West

had to be brought to its knees as rapidly as possible. To accomplish this, Sherman devised the first major use of psychological warfare. Whereas Grant's strategy was to hammer away at an opposing army, Sherman thought more in geographical terms. He would strike at enemy cities, fields, and facilities; he would break the Confederacy's will to resist by slashing through the very heart of the South.

By early May, Sherman was poised east of Chattanooga with three armies, totaling about 112,000 veteran soldiers. The ill-equipped Confederate army, now under defensive genius Joseph E. Johnston, numbered approximately 60,000

The 21st Michigan, a regiment that marched with Sherman. (*NA*)

Sherman makes his futile assault on Johnston's impregnable position on Kennesaw Mountain. Painting by Thure de Thulstrup.

men. Johnston's position was at Dalton, Georgia, astride the Atlanta-Chattanooga railroad. Sherman's plan was to move down that line toward Atlanta and to extend the Federal right beyond Johnston's power to resist. Thus caught in the vise of attack from north and west, the small Confederate army would be shattered. The valuable railroad and industrial center of Atlanta would then surrender, and the Deep South would be at Sherman's mercy.

Combating Sherman's offensive, while on the short end of 2 to 1 odds, required all of Johnston's defensive skill. He fell back to Resaca in the face of Sherman's two-pronged advance. During May 13-16, Johnston held fast at Resaca against several Federal assaults. The two armies suffered about 5,500 losses each before a Federal flanking movement again forced the Confederates into retreat through the mountain passes to the west.

Heavy skirmishing followed at Adairsville, Kingston, and Cassville. Johnston continued to wage delaying actions until Federal flanking columns threatened his rear. Then he would make an orderly retirement—always destroying bridges and railroads as he went. A series of heavy clashes at Dallas (May

25-28) delayed but did not deter Sherman's advance. On June 27, Sherman abandoned a flank maneuver and sent three divisions in a headlong, direct assault against Johnston on the slopes of Kennesaw Mountain. Entrenched, determined Confederates were more than a match for Union courage: Sherman suffered nearly 3,000 casualties to Johnston's 500-700. The Federal commander resorted again to turning movements and, early in July, drove Johnston into the trenches of Atlanta.

Confederate officials in Richmond were unimpressed with Johnston's skillful use of inferior numbers. They saw only that Sherman was now at Atlanta's doorstep. So Johnston on July 17 was removed from command and replaced by General John B. Hood.

Lieutenant General
John Bell Hood. He replaced
Johnston's caution
with rash attack. (*LC*)

Sherman (center) inspects Union
siege lines before Atlanta.
Painting by Thure de Thulstrup.

View of Atlanta after its surrender. (*NA*)

Sherman had good reason to be "pleased at this change." Hood's valor (he had lost a leg and the use of an arm in earlier battles) overshadowed a lack of skill and caution. These defects Hood quickly demonstrated by launching a July 20 attack on Sherman at Peachtree Creek that accomplished nothing but the loss of 2,500-3,000 irreplaceable Southern troops. Two days later, Hood attacked anew east of Atlanta. Again he was repulsed, this time with 8,500 casualties. Sherman then extended the Federal lines slowly around Atlanta. By the end of August the Federals were on the verge of cutting the last rail link to the city. Hood attacked desperately at Jonesboro but was easily beaten back. The Confederates evacuated Atlanta on September 1, and Sherman's army marched triumphantly into the city the following day.

The effects of the fall of Atlanta can hardly be exaggerated. For the Confederacy, it meant the loss of the Deep South's most important rail center; and it foretold intense destructions yet to come. Conversely, the seizure of Atlanta was a tremendous boost to Northern morale sagging from "Grant's butchery" and setbacks elsewhere. It assured the re-election of Lincoln and Republicans dedicated to carrying the war to a successful conclusion.

Confederate successes in the West paled appreciably when compared to the loss of Atlanta.

In the spring of 1864, Confederates in the Trans-Mississippi theater dealt General Nathaniel P. Banks his worst—and final—defeat. Indeed, Banks's last campaign, known as the Red River Expedition, was one of the costliest fiascos of the war. Two factors prompted the campaign: Federal desire to seize large quantities of cotton so valuable to Northern and European mills, and the need to strengthen the Union's control over Louisiana and east Texas by securing Shreveport, Louisiana and the adjacent countryside.

The Federal effort was a joint land-and-water operation under Banks and Admiral David D. Porter. The armada included 30,000 troops, 20 warships, and double that number of transport vessels. Only 15,000 scattered Confederates offered any obstacle. The campaign began March 12 and ended May 21; in every respect for the North, it was an utter failure. Southerners burned $60,000,000 worth of cotton to prevent its capture; Banks suffered inglorious defeats at Sabine Cross Roads and Pleasant Hill; the fleet floundered for miles in the turbid Red River, constantly under harassment from sharpshooters; bitter quarrels erupted among the officers as morale in the ranks melted.

Total Federal losses were 8,162 men, nine ships (including three gunboats), 57 guns, and 822 wagons loaded with supplies. The campaign deprived Sherman's army of additional manpower, delayed the capture of Mobile by ten months, and enabled Kirby Smith's Confederates in the Trans-Mississippi to hold out for another year. Banks was speedily removed from command.

Admiral David D. Porter almost lost his fleet in the Red River Campaign. (*LC*)

That spring, too, the Confederate "Wizard of the Saddle" was active. Nathan Bedford Forrest was an uneducated cavalry leader who nevertheless exhibited an intuitive genius that made him one of the leading captains in the Civil War. On April 12, Forrest's men stormed the Federal garrison at Fort Pillow, Tennessee. The alleged "massacre" that followed remains one of the most controversial incidents of the 1860's. The Federal push into Georgia a month later sent "Old Bedford" on a rampage through Tennessee and northern Mississippi. Sherman then dispatched a heavy force under boastful Samuel D. Sturgis to take care of Forrest once and for all. Sturgis' command numbered 8,300 men, 22 guns and 250 wagons. Forrest had at his disposal less than half that strength.

Nine days after leaving Memphis, on June 10th, the Federal expedition met Forrest—and disaster—at Brice's Cross Roads. The Confederate attacks were so sudden and severe, Sturgis reported, that "order gave way to confusion, and confusion to panic." What was left of the Federal command made the return trip to Memphis in two and half days. Sturgis lost 2,240 men, 16 guns, 176 wagons, 1,500 small arms, and 300,000 rounds of ammunition.

The fall of Atlanta in September was but an intermediate step in Sherman's strategy. Not until the Confederacy was viciously cut in half would he consider his campaign successful. "You cannot glorify war in harsher terms than I will," Sherman warned. "War is cruelty, and you cannot refine it."

When Hood's skeleton regiments moved from Atlanta to Tennessee to threaten Sherman's rear bases of supply, the Federal general refused to take the bait. He sent part of his army under George H. Thomas to check the Confederate threat. With the remainder of his force—60,000 soldiers, Sherman cut his traces, marched away from Hood, and struck for the sea. On November 16, leaving Atlanta in flames, Sherman's army headed eastward in two columns toward the ocean.

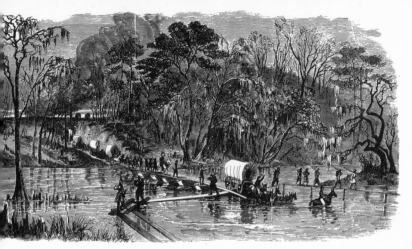

Sherman's March to the Sea. Crossing the Edisto River.

Sherman purposefully kept his wings spread wide. No Confederate forces of any size stood in his path. Hence, his troops could—and did—cut a swath of destruction forty to sixty miles wide. Union forces easily occupied the state capital of Milledgeville and held a mock session of the Georgia legislature. In the course of the march, plundering occurred with an alarming thoroughness; anything that would prove beneficial to the Confederate cause was taken or destroyed. Sherman himself estimated the total damage at $100,000,000. The "March to the Sea" became one of the most brutal episodes of the entire war. Yet it achieved its purpose. When Sherman on December 22 reached his destination and presented Savannah to Lincoln as a "Christmas-gift," morale and determined resistance in the Deep South were dead.

By then the same plight had befallen the once-proud Army of Tennessee. Hood's forces drove into Tennessee and, on November 30, encountered part of Thomas' command at Franklin. The aggressive Hood was convinced that the Army of Tennessee under Johnston had forgotten how to attack. He rashly ordered his troops to charge across mile-wide open fields without artillery support. The result was a slaughter: over 6,000 Confederates killed or wounded, among whom

Sherman reviews his army in Savannah, January 1865. William Waud drawing. (*LC*)

were five generals killed and one mortally wounded, and more than fifty regimental colonels. Still Hood stubbornly persevered. He moved to Nashville and made a weak siege of that city, giving Thomas the time to collect his full army. On December 15-16, Thomas delivered a series of heavy assaults on the Southern positions. Hood's lines snapped as Union forces gained "one of the most smashing victories of the war." The 13,200 Southern casualties represented half of Hood's army. Those Confederates who survived trudged southward in defeat, singing with wry humor of how "The gallant Hood of Texas played hell in Tennessee."

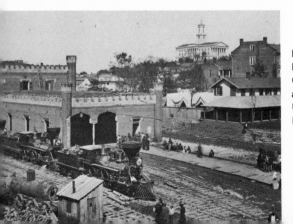

Railroad yard at Nashville, Tennessee. Cars and locomotives are units of the United States Military Railroad. (*LC*)

By spring of the war's fourth year, the Army of Northern Virginia was in critical condition. Federal thrusts at the weak Confederate lines during the nine-month siege had drained much from "Lee's Miserables." Sharp clashes, such as occurred at Reams's Station, Deep Bottom, Globe Tavern, Boydton Plank Road, Tom's Brook, Weldon Railroad, and Hatcher's Run, reduced Lee's ranks and tightened the Federal noose. Sickness, malnutrition, and lack of clothing accentuated the suffering. Desertion among Confederate units jumped dangerously. In February, morning reports for Lee's army "became a sickening and bewildering story of desertion"— as attested by a ten-day period in which 1,094 Southerners

1865 in the East

disappeared from the Petersburg trenches.

On March 2, Sheridan captured most of Early's Valley command at Waynesboro and then destroyed the Virginia Central Railroad as he rode eastward to join Grant. Lee realized that a climax was now approaching—just as Grant

became fully determined not to allow Lee to escape from the Petersburg line. On March 25, Lee made a strong attack at Fort Stedman. The onslaught was intended either to break Grant's tight hold or to be at least a diversion while Lee readied the rest of his army for withdrawal. Federal troops repelled the assaults with losses to Lee of 4,500 men.

Grant now delivered the blow for which he had been preparing for months. On April 1, Federal infantry and cavalry

Sheridan's charge at the Battle of Five Forks.

crushed the Southern position at Five Forks, seventeen miles southwest of Petersburg; and the following day Grant's entire forty-mile front surged forward. The Confederate line bent in several places, then snapped into fragments. Lee abandoned Petersburg and Richmond (both of which were promptly occupied by elements of Grant's army) and retreated westward. The long siege had cost the Federals 42,000 casualties. However, Lee's 28,000 losses during those nine months had reduced the Confederate army to a skeleton no more than one fourth the size of Grant's forces.

Confederate strategy was to follow the route of the Richmond & Danville Railroad. Lee wished to use this one remaining line as a source for badly needed supplies. Then, if

Fire swept Richmond after its surrender.
On the skyline, the Capitol. (*LC*)

his army could reach Danville, it had a chance of uniting with the Army of Tennessee; together they might withstand Grant's punishing blows. All of this proved to be a forlorn hope. When Lee's footsore, half-starved men reached the railroad at Amelia Court House, they found not boxcars loaded with food but empty tracks. A supply train from Danville had mysteriously continued on to Richmond —and been captured. Forage parties, hastily dispatched into the countryside by Lee, brought back only the news of a citizenry equally impoverished.

Now Lee could only trust that his smaller force might be able to outdistance the great hordes moving after him. But on April 5, Sheridan's cavalry swung into the Confederates' path and compelled Lee to veer northwestward toward Lynchburg. The next day almost a third of the Confederate army

Union soldiers tramp past the blazing ruins of Richmond, jubilantly greeted by Negroes.

The last of Ewell's corps surrenders at Sayler's Creek.

was trapped at Sayler's Creek. Lacking artillery and an escape route, 8,000 disheartened Rebels surrendered. The remainder of Lee's ragged army plodded wearily on, somehow managing to endure painful skirmishes at Farmville and High Bridge. On the night of April 8, artillery flashes and the glow of campfires revealed the worst to Lee: Grant's rapidly moving army had blocked all escape avenues.

Around 2 p.m. on Palm Sunday, April 9, Lee and Grant met in the front parlor of Wilmer McLean's Appomattox farmhouse. Grant proposed extremely generous terms that included allowing paroled Confederate soldiers to retain their mounts for the spring plowing they would shortly need to do. Lee accepted the terms with a mixture of gratitude and despair.

The McLean House, Appomattox. (*LC*)

The actual surrender ceremony occurred on April 12, when 28,231 exhausted Confederates representing the Army of Northern Virginia relinquished their arms and battle flags. A Federal general, deeply moved by the scene, described it as "an awed stillness, and breath-holding, as if it were the passing of the dead."

The surrender scene, sketched by Walton Tabor.

1865 in the West

Sherman gave his men a month's rest at Savannah before resuming his surgery of the South. The resultant "March Through the Carolinas" was like a "devouring flame" to a Confederacy already near death.

On February 1, the 60,000 battle-hardened bluecoats again abandoned their supply lines and slashed into South Carolina. Sherman was content to leave the remaining Confederate coastal fortresses to Union naval and amphibious forces, which captured Fort Fisher that month and thereby closed the last major Confederate access to the sea. Charleston likewise fell to the U.S. Navy on the day (February 17) after Sherman left Columbia, the capital of the Palmetto State, in flames.

Robert E. Lee, belatedly named General in Chief of Confederate military forces, reinstated Joseph E. Johnston as commander of the Army of Tennessee. Johnston moved into North Carolina from Mississippi to try to contain Sherman. His fragmentary regiments totaled about 18,000 men—a pitiful shadow of a once-proud army. Sherman's veterans occupied Fayetteville and its valuable arsenal on March 10, then turned eastward toward the important rail junction of Goldsboro.

Johnston now made a do-or-die gamble: He concentrated his meager forces at Bentonville and savagely attacked Sherman's left wing, hoping to force Sherman's withdrawal by defeating in turn the two Federal lines of advance. The battle of Bentonville raged for three days (March 19-21); on the third day, Sherman's two wings united and drove Johnston from the field. Sherman's occupation of Goldsboro shortly thereafter ended the great "march."

Lee's surrender at Appomattox two weeks later left Johnston's battered army completely alone. Yet a Sherman terrible in war proved to be a man compassionate in victory. His initial surrender terms to Johnston were so generous that Washington authorities rejected them and directed Sherman to re-negotiate. On April 26, at the Bennett house near Durham, Johnston signed the revised terms. His army had been reduced by deaths, wounds, and desertion in the final days to about 10,000 men.

Other Confederate armies throughout the South soon furled their banners. Early in April, three divisions of Federal cavalry under General James H. Wilson overwhelmed Bedford Forrest's troopers at Selma, Alabama. Wilson reported inflicting 1,200 Southern casualties and taking 6,820 prisoners. The few survivors of Forrest's command joined General Richard Taylor's army, which in turn surrendered May 4 at Citronelle, Alabama to General Edward R. S. Canby's forces. The Confederacy's last significant army, under Kirby Smith, laid down its arms May 26 at New Orleans.

By then Lincoln was dead from an assassin's bullet, the Southern states were prostrate from four years of destruction, the cream of American manhood had been slain, a heritage

Columbia, South
Carolina, after Sherman's
troops passed through. (*NA*)

Johnston (left) and Sherman discussing surrender
terms at the Bennett house.

of hate had been planted in many quarters, and the old Union
that men had sought to preserve had been irrevocably shattered and replaced by a new one.

The War on the Sea

During the American Revolution, George Washington stated a basic tenet of military strategy: "In any operation, and under all circumstances, a decisive naval superiority is to be considered as a fundamental principle, and the basis upon which every hope of success must ultimately depend." This axiom applied pointedly to the Civil War, for Union naval power in the 1860's proved so important that its effects on the defeat of the Confederacy can hardly be exaggerated.

The U.S. Navy faced an awesome dilemma at war's outset, when Lincoln proclaimed a blockade of the South. The Navy had but a handful of ships available to isolate the 3,500 miles of Confederate seacoast. Both sides realized how absolutely dependent the Southern nation was on European sources of supplies. For the North to win the war, an effective blockade was imperative. The Navy was also needed for military operations along the coast and in the rivers, as well as for the protection of American commercial vessels at sea.

The very presence of the Navy in the war's first weeks had a substantial effect on the outcome. Federal cruisers in the Potomac River and Chesapeake Bay in 1861 probably saved Washington, D.C. and Maryland from falling into the hands of the Confederacy, and there can be little doubt that Federal naval control of the upper Mississippi and Ohio Rivers helped to keep Kentucky and Missouri in the Union.

The Navy Yard at Brooklyn, New York, June 1861.

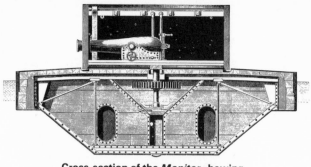

Cross-section of the *Monitor* showing turret-moving machinery. (*B&L*)

It is a testimonial to Lincoln's hardworking Secretary of the Navy, Gideon Welles, that Northern strength afloat became as highly potent and effective as it did. While the few ships at hand began blockading the major Southern ports in 1861 (and captured 150 blockade-runners that first year), Welles and his equally brilliant assistant, Gustavus V. Fox, worked indefatigably to build a mighty sea force. Construction and purchase of craft continued at a rapid pace as Welles secured every type of ship "from Captain Noah to Captain Cook." From only forty-two serviceable vessels in 1861, the Navy reached 671 ships by 1864. Many of these were so radically new in design and performance that the Civil War truly ushered in the modern era of naval power.

The *Monitor* is an excellent case in point. Invented by John Ericcson and constructed during the winter of 1861-1862, this revolutionary vessel possessed a number of startling innovations. It was a small, all-iron ship, with its hull only inches above the water line. On its deck were but two superstructures: a revolving gun turret that could withstand a ten-inch shell at close range, and a small pilothouse. High maneuverability was one of its chief tactical advantages.

The famous 1862 *Monitor-Virginia* **duel** has already been summarized. Neither ship emerged victorious from the Hampton Roads confrontation. Yet the fact that the *Monitor* held its own against the larger, more ominous looking, *Virginia* did

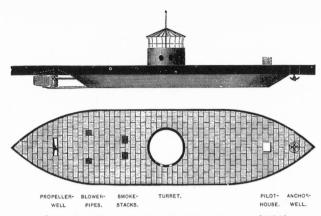

| PROPELLER-
WELL | BLOWER-
PIPES. | SMOKE-
STACKS. | TURRET. | PILOT-
HOUSE. | ANCHOR-
WELL. |

Side elevation and deck plan of the *Monitor*. (*B&L*)

"Powder monkey"
on deck of USS
New Hampshire. (LC)

Lincoln's efficient
Secretary
of the Navy
Gideon Welles. (*LC*)

much to dash Confederate hopes of a naval super-weapon. A few weeks later, the *Virginia* was run aground and burned to prevent its capture by the fleet that accompanied McClellan's army to the Peninsula. The original *Monitor* was also ill-fated. On the night of December 30-31, 1862, it sank in a storm off Cape Hatteras, North Carolina. Extensive but futile efforts were made during the recent Civil War Centennial to locate the wreckage.

Increasingly effective as the blockade was, Lincoln and Secretary Welles did not regard it as sufficient alone to cut the South's commercial strings with foreign markets. Occupation of key points along the seacoast would strengthen the blockade, jeopardize those ports still open, give the Navy fueling stations closer to the areas of operation, and enable fleets to move in greater concentration against the remaining prime targets.

Such "hop-scotch" tactics began in August 1861, when an amphibious expedition secured Forts Clark and Hatteras on the North Carolina coast. These captures put a stop to Confederate privateering in the area. Two months later, Flag Officer Samuel F. DuPont commanded Federal forces in the capture of Port Royal, South Carolina, giving the Union control of the town of Beaufort and the vital sea islands nearby, plus a needed naval base deep in the South. During February-March 1862, General Ambrose E. Burnside led a heavy armada that overpowered the Confederate defenses at Roanoke Island. The fall of this strategic bastion led to the Union occupation of the North Carolina coastal towns of New Berne, Edenton, and Elizabeth City—and in addition, left the Carolina interior vulnerable to attack. The capture of Fort Pulaski in April all but closed the Savannah River and Georgia's leading seaport. The recapture of Norfolk, also that spring, sealed the Virginia coast.

By 1864, the Confederacy held but four of its major ports: Charleston, South Carolina; Mobile, Alabama; Wilmington, North Carolina; and Galveston, Texas. They became the focal points for Federal naval attacks in the war's last year.

A Charleston fort
replies to
Farragut's ironclads.
(*Illus. London News*)

Admiral John A.
Dahlgren (*KA*)

Farragut's fleet in Mobile Bay. CSS *Tennessee* in foreground.

Assault on Fort Fisher. Painting by J. O. Davidson.

Charleston, "the seedbed of the Confederacy," proved especially thorny. For 587 consecutive days in 1863-1864, the city was besieged by fleets under DuPont and Admiral John A. Dahlgren. Southern batteries played havoc with monitors, gunboats, and frigates that ventured into range. Union amphibious assaults against outlying works were likewise unsuccessful. The proud fortress-city stood battered but defiant until February 1865, when the approach of Sherman's army led to its fall. Charleston's long stand in the face of seemingly overpowering Federal might is one of the heroic sagas of the Confederacy.

Mobile became the South's chief gulf port after the April 1862 fall of New Orleans, and Confederates strengthened it accordingly with shore forts, underwater mines (known then as "torpedoes"), and a fleet spearheaded by the deadly ram *Tennessee*. The Federal navy prepared carefully until August 5, 1864, when "the Victor of New Orleans" struck again. Crusty David G. Farragut led his fleet of ironclads and frigates up the dangerous channel. Confederate artillery raked the Union warships and inflicted heavy damage. Yet Farragut, lashed to the rigging of the flagship *Hartford*, refused to turn back. Whether Farragut actually shouted "Damn the torpedoes! Full speed ahead!" is debatable. Nevertheless, he steamed into Mobile Bay and achieved one of the paramount naval victories of the war.

The Confederacy's last Atlantic opening was Wilmington, situated several miles up the Cape Fear River. Powerful Fort Fisher, guarding the river's junction with the sea, was the key to Wilmington itself. Confederates inside the fort repulsed a December 1864 land-and-sea assault by forces under General Benjamin F. Butler and Admiral David D. Porter. The following month, Porter's fleet and 8,000 Federal infantrymen under General Alfred H. Terry silenced the guns of Fort Fisher and overran the works. The fall of Wilmington ended Confederate blockade-running.

Typical Mississippi warship, the USS *Cairo*. (*LC*)

"The Blockade Runner Ashore." Painting by D. J. Kennedy.

Galveston, Texas held out until after the end. Located on the frontier of the Confederacy, it never became a principal object for attack as did New Orleans, Charleston, and Mobile. On June 2, 1865, almost two months after Appomattox, the city officially capitulated to Union authorities.

Of equal or possibly greater importance than Federal naval efforts at sea was the work done by the various river squadrons and fleets working in conjunction with Union armies. In many of the war's major campaigns, Federal armies followed waterways and depended upon them for support, logistics, and a safe retreat if necessary. Much of the story of the war in the West can be told in terms of joint army and navy operations. Ulysses S. Grant, more than any other general in the Civil War, realized the full potential of sea power—and made the most use of it. His first campaign, at Belmont, Missouri, was largely amphibious. Grant's drives against Forts Henry and Donelson were successful only because he utilized ships for rapid transportation of soldiers and because the Union gunboats gave him "inland control of the sea" by proving more than a match for Southern shore batteries. Federal warships protected Grant's flank on the drive through Tennessee, and salvos from those gunboats were a large factor in Grant's victorious counterattack at Shiloh. The North's final investment of Vicksburg, and ultimate control of the Mississippi River, could not have resulted but for the floating firepower of the U. S. Navy.

Similarly, McClellan's entire 1862 Peninsular Campaign depended upon naval support. His huge Army of the Potomac could not have disembarked at Fortress Monroe if the menace of the *Virginia* had not been checked by the *Monitor*. Federal squadrons on the James River paralleled McClellan's advance on Richmond and gave constant protection to his left flank. When Lee's counteroffensive at the Seven Days crumbled the Federal right, McClellan was saved from disaster by retreating to the James, where he had both the protective batteries of naval gunboats and a secure line of logistics by water. McClellan's dilemma and eventual salvation by the Navy was the "Dunkirk" of the war.

Two years later, when Grant was hammering futilely in front of Richmond, he was able to shift across the James and move on Petersburg because Federal ships controlled all waterways to the east. The U. S. Navy made possible the climactic, nine-month siege that followed. It alone insured during those months the food and equipment for Grant's enormous army. How vital Grant considered the Navy is best revealed by his fears when Confederate ironclads late in 1864 attempted to break the James River supply line.

The Southern Confederacy had no real navy and never acquired the facilities for building one. Stephen R. Mallory, the Confederate naval secretary, was unable to surmount the additional obstacles of obtaining enough funds for sufficient foreign purchases and of overcoming the North's superior overseas diplomacy. Confederate naval efforts were thus restricted to privateering, blockade-running, menacing Union commercial ships on the high seas, and to a series of revolutionary counter-weapons such as mines, torpedoes, and tactical submarines.

Confederate Secretary of the Navy Stephen R. Mallory accomplished much with little.

Rear Admiral Raphael Semmes CSN. His *Alabama* became the bane of Northern shipping. (*LC*)

What glory the Confederacy achieved at sea came from a score of cruisers that, under adventuresome crews, preyed singly on Federal naval and maritime vessels. This had the dual effect of drawing Federal warships from blockade duty (thereby increasing the odds for blockade-runners) and of denting Northern commercial interests. The first of such sleek raiders was the 500-ton steamer *Sumter*. Her commander was Raphael Semmes, the Confederacy's most brilliant sailor. A native of Alabama, Semmes had a quarter-century's naval experience behind him when civil war began. He captained the *Sumter* for only six months, yet during that period the cruiser captured eighteen Federal ships in the Atlantic and Caribbean.

On August 24, 1862, Semmes took command of the South's premier cruiser, the *Alabama*. This 1000-ton steamer was equipped with eight guns and two 300-horsepower engines. Its crew of 144 men included more English sympathizers than Confederate seamen. During its two-year reign of terror on the high seas, the *Alabama* came to be regarded as a ghost ship. It ranged from Newfoundland to Singapore, always appearing as if from nowhere to assail its victims. The *Alabama's* sixty-nine prizes included the USS *Hatteras*, which she sank after capture.

The Confederate cruiser destroyed more than $10,000,000 worth of Federal shipping and literally drove the American merchant marine to cover. But on June 19, 1864, the *Alabama* was cornered off the coast of France by the USS *Kearsarge*. For an hour, the two vessels exchanged broadsides at a range of 900 yards. The *Alabama* sank with twenty-six hands; the remainder were picked from the sea by the *Kearsarge* and nearby European vessels that had witnessed the classic battle.

The CSS *Florida*, under Captain John Newland Maffitt, was a privateer that seized thirty-seven prizes during eighteen months of cruising in the Caribbean and South Atlantic. Her capture in a Brazilian seaport by the USS *Wachusetts* was a

Union sailors relax on deck of warship with games and music. (*NA*)

The *Kearsarge* (right) meets the *Alabama*. Painting by J. O. Davidson.

violation of neutral rights that the United States later disavowed. The *Tallahassee*, a former blockade-runner operating out of Wilmington, took thirty-nine prizes during her 1864 saga. Last of the Confederate cruisers was the fabled *Shenandoah*, a sailing steamer under Captain James I. Waddell. The raider sailed from England in October 1864 to disrupt the Northern whaling fleet in the Bering Sea. Among the *Shenandoah's* forty-eight captures were eight whalers burned collectively two months after Appomattox. When Captain Waddell learned of the war's termination, he returned to Liverpool. There, on November 6, 1865, the last Confederate naval ensign was furled.

Confederate blockade-runners provided some of the highest drama in the Civil War. A typical blockade-runner was a lean, low, paddle-wheel steamer, painted a dull gray and burning almost smokeless anthracite coal. Having telescope smokestacks and other streamlined features, these sleek vessels were capable of speeds up to fifteen knots. Their usual tactic, when approaching the southern coast with a full cargo, was to keep out of sight until nightfall. Then the vessel would make a dash for port in the darkness. Confederate coastal guns would lay down a heavy bombardment on Federal blockaders while the vessel was making its run for safety. If the ship were severely damaged by Federal gunfire, it was deliberately run ashore so that at least part of its cargo could be salvaged.

The Confederacy devised several novel weapons for use in coastal defense. Various types of water mines were developed but never proved highly effective. In January 1863, Texas soldiers fortified some merchant steamers with bales of cotton on the decks and launched attacks on blockading squadrons. At Galveston the "cotton-clad" fleet captured the USS *Harriet Lane* and routed half a dozen other blockaders. The strange-looking flotilla moved on to Sabine Pass and seized two other Union warships before Federal naval reinforcements arrived.

Experimentation by the South with "torpedo boats" centered around the *David*, constructed at Charleston in the autumn of 1863. The *David* was a small, cigar-shaped vessel, propelled by steam. It cruised almost submerged and attacked by means of a torpedo attached to a long spar projecting from the bow. Thus armed, the *David* did extensive damage to the blockader *New Ironsides* before running aground at Charleston.

Unique among Confederate naval innovations was history's first tactical submarine, the *H. L. Hunley*. Its short career is a story of perseverance in the face of repeated failure.

Designed and financed by Horace L. Hunley, the submarine was built in the spring of 1863 at Mobile. The vessel sank on its initial trial run, but all hands escaped. The Confederate Government showed no interest in the enterprise. Hunley thereupon enlisted private financial support for the construction of a second submarine, which was completed that summer and shipped by rail to Charleston. On its first trial run there, a passing ship flooded the open hatches and sent the *Hunley* to the bottom of the harbor with a loss of eight of nine crewmen. The ship was raised and repaired—only to go down again three weeks later from a similar accident. Six seamen perished in that disaster.

Again the vessel was brought to the surface. Hunley then assumed personal command for an experimental attack run. The designer intended to dive beneath the CSS *Indian Chief* and have a dummy torpedo being pulled by a line strike the *Indian Chief's* hull. Midway through the run, the *Hunley's* ballast tanks burst. Hunley and eight crewmen drowned. The vessel was brought to the surface several days later and its occupants interred with military honors in Charleston.

Confederate "submarine infernal machine" intended to destroy the *Minnesota*. Apparently this was a two-man, man-power operated craft. (*U.S. Navy photo*)

A volunteer crew under Lieutenant George E. Dixon then took the *Hunley* into action. On the night of February 17, 1864, with a torpedo attached to a bow spar, the *Hunley* moved among the Federal blockading fleet and sank the USS *Housatonic*, the world's first victim of submarine attack. However, the *Hunley* also sank in the explosion, with a loss of all hands. No trace of the vessel has ever been found.

The South's many land forts and shore batteries were no match for the heavy and mobile firepower that the U. S. Navy brought to bear against the Confederacy. While the C. S. Navy had daring officers and courageous seamen, it never had the materiel necessary to mount a force sufficiently strong to challenge its Northern counterpart. On the basis of what was accomplished in the face of almost no resources, Confederate naval undertaking must be judged as little short of miraculous.

In the end, however, the effect of the U. S. Navy was overwhelming. President Lincoln spoke for posterity when he observed during the war: "Nor must Uncle Sam's web feet be forgotten. At all of the watery margins they have been present. Not only on the deep sea, the broad bay, the rapid river, but also up the narrow, muddy bayou, and wherever the ground was a little damp, they have been and made their mark."

Submarine *H. L. Hunley*, from painting by Conrad Wise Chapman. Courtesy The Boston Athenaeum.

The Heritage of a Civil War

These men made their final payment for the war. The Union
cemetery at City Point, Virginia. Note the number of unmarked
graves. (*NA*)

One of every five participants in the Civil War died in service. While 126,000 Americans died in World War I and 407,000 in World War II, more than 618,000 Americans were victims of the Civil War. The North lost a total of 360,-022 men, of whom 67,058 were killed in action and 43,012 died of battle wounds. Extant records for the Confederacy do not provide complete statistics, yet certainly about 258,000 Southern soldiers died of all causes in the war. Approximately 94,000 of these were battle fatalities.

The biggest killers of troops in the 1860's were not bullets and shells but sickness and disease. Some 400,000 men perished from such maladies as diarrhea, dysentery, measles, smallpox, chicken pox, typhoid fever, pneumonia, and gangrene. Intestinal disorders alone killed more than 57,000 Federal soldiers. Since proper food and sanitation were even more lacking on the Confederate side, the number of deaths among Southern troops from diarrhea and associated illnesses was proportionately higher. But the suffering does not stop there. At least 1,000,000 men were seriously wounded or severely ill during the war. Unquestionably, lingering effects of these disablements continued in most cases for years after the fighting ceased.

Human loss cannot be measured in terms of dollars. Materially speaking, the war cost the United States more than $15,000,000,000 in property destroyed, fields burned bare, materiel expended, and institutions both created and eliminated. The price tags of America's legacy of such items as a

Union wounded at a field hospital at Savage Station during the Seven Days' battles on the Peninsula. (*LC*)

ruined South, military occupation, years of political corruption directly attributable to the war, partisan excesses, discrimination, and intolerance can never be computed.

The heritage of hate that the Civil War engendered mellowed appreciably with the passage of time. Veterans on both sides periodically gathered at the great battle sites to relive deeds of daring and to exchange anecdotes and compliments with former enemies. Their ability to forgive was an inspiration to future generations. In time, the whole nation came to revere the final survivors of the struggle. The last "Billy Yank," Albert Woolson of Duluth, Minnesota, died August 2, 1956, at the age of 109. The last "Johnny Reb," 117-year-old Walter Williams of Houston, Texas, died December 19, 1959.

The Civil War holds undying fascination for people all over the world. Americans have probably read more about the war than the rest of man's history combined. More than 60,000 books and articles have appeared since the gunsmoke cleared, and the stream of literary works shows no sign of drying up. For the Civil War was "our" war. It pitted American against American, brother against brother, father

Confederate dead in the Sunken Road at Fredericksburg after Sedgwick's assault on May 3, 1863.

against son. The deeds of valor and sacrifice performed countless times by either Blue or Gray are heroics in which all Americans can take pride.

Moreover, the lines of dissension were never quite clear. Contestants in most wars appear vividly as either black or white. Yet the whole Civil War seemed to hover in gray shadows. Each side maintained that it was fighting for the America envisioned by the Founding Fathers. Delaware, a slave state, remained in the Union; antislaveryites Robert E. Lee and "Stonewall" Jackson fought for the Confederacy. In 1861, future Confederate generals Joseph E. Johnston and James Longstreet were serving in the U. S. Army—while future Union general William T. Sherman was living in the South. Mrs. Abraham Lincoln had two brothers and a brother-in-law who gave their lives fighting under the Stars and Bars.

Captain James S. West CSA.

No nation has ever fought itself and, a scant 100 years later, been bound by so many ties of nationalism and brotherhood as now characterize America. The progress of the United States, after a war that would seem to have left wounds too deep for healing, is a memorial to Americans of every age and creed who were willing to bind up the nation's wounds and march ahead confidently into the future. A United States forged in the death and steel of Civil War battles continued its growth, developed its destiny, and ultimately fulfilled Lincoln's vision of an America that is "that last great hope of earth."

Home from the war. (*LC*)

"With Fate Against Them" is the title Gilbert Gaul gave this painting of a Confederate line of battle.

Sergeant Oscar Ryder, 7th Regiment, N.Y.S.M.

RECOMMENDED READINGS

The following is a list of readings which Dr. Robertson suggests for more on a variety of facets of the great Civil War:

Andrews, J. Cutler, *The North Reports the Civil War* (1955)

―――――, *The South Reports the Civil War* (1970)

Catton, Bruce, *The Centennial History of the Civil War* (3 vols., 1962-1965)

Cornish, Dudley T., *The Sable Arm* (1956)

Coulter, E. Merton, *The Confederate States of America, 1861-1865* (1950)

Craven, Avery O., *The Coming of the Civil War* (1957)

Foote, Shelby, *The Civil War* (2 vols., 1958-1963)

Freeman, Douglas S., *Lee's Lieutenants* (3 vols., 1942-1944)

―――――, *R. E. Lee* (4 vols., 1934-1935)

Hassler, Warren W., Jr., *Commanders of the Army of the Potomac* (1962)

Horn, Stanley F., *The Army of Tennessee* (1953)

Johnson, James R., *Horsemen Blue and Gray* (1960)

Johnson, Robert U., and Buel, C. C. (eds.), *Battles and Leaders of the Civil War* (4 vols., 1958-1959)

Jones, Virgil C., *The Civil War at Sea* (3 vols., 1960-1962)

Ketchum, Richard M., *The American Heritage Picture Book of the Civil War* (1960)

Leech, Margaret, *Reveille in Washington* (1941)

Lord, Francis A., *Civil War Collector's Encyclopedia* (1963)

―――――, *They Fought for the Union* (1960)

Massey, Mary Elizabeth, *Bonnet Brigades* (1966)

Miller, Francis T., *The Photographic History of the Civil War* (10 vols., 1957)

Nevins, Allan, *et. al.* (eds.), *Civil War Books: A Critical Bibliography* (2 vols., 1967-1969)

―――――, *War for the Union* (2 vols., 1959-1960)

Randall, James G., and Donald, David, *The Civil War and Reconstruction* (1961)

Robertson, James I., Jr., *The Stonewall Brigade* (1963)

Stampp, Kenneth P., *And the War Came* (1959)

Thomas, Benjamin P., *Abraham Lincoln* (1952)

U. S. Navy History Division, *Civil War Naval Chronology* (6 vols., 1961-1966)

Vandiver, Frank E., *Their Tattered Flags* (1970)

Wiley, Bell I., *Embattled Confederates* (1964)

―――――, *They Who Fought Here* (1960)

Williams, Kenneth P., *Lincoln Finds a General* (5 vols., 1949-1959)

Williams, T. Harry, *Lincoln and His Generals* (1952)

Index

(Italicized entries refer to illustrations)

Design by Krone Art Service, Inc. / Composition by Caxton Co. / Printing by The Telegraph Press

IMPORTANT BATTLES OF THE CIVIL WAR

State Capitals are lettered thus RALEIGH. *Battles are indicated by stars; those in the neighborhood of cities and larger towns thus* ☆, *and those at other places.* ★

STATUTE MILES
0   50   100   150   200

MISSOURI
ILLINOIS
INDIANA
INDIANAPOLIS
CINCIN

LEXINGTON
JEFFERSON CITY
ST LOUIS
Missouri R.
Mississippi R.
Ohio R.
LOUISVILLE
FRANKF
LEXINGTO

CARTHAGE
WILSON'S CREEK
CAIRO
PADUCAH
Green R.
PERRYVILLE
KENTU

PEA RIDGE
BELMONT
NEWMADRID
COLUMBUS
ISLAND No 10
FT HENRY
FT DONELSON
BOWLING GREEN
MILL SPRIN
CUM

White R.
Arkansas R.
TENNESSEE
Cumberland R.
NASHVILLE
KNOXV

ARKANSAS
LITTLE ROCK
HELENA
MEMPHIS
SHILOH OR
PITTSBURG LDG.
SAVANNAH
FRANKLIN
MURFREESBORO
Tennessee R.
LOOKOUT MT
CHATTANOOGA
CHICKAMAUGA
RINGGOLD

HOLLY SPRINGS
CORINTH
IUKA
DECATUR
Tallahatchie R.
RESACA
CASSVILLE
ALLATO
ROME
KENN
MAR
Wachita R.
Yazoo R.
FT PEMBERTON
Black Warrior R.
DALLAS
ATLANTA
GE
AND

SHREVEPORT
LOUISIANA
MISSISSIPPI
ALABAMA
WEST POINT
SABIN X ROADS
VICKSBURG
JACKSON
MONTGOMERY
Alabama R.
Chattahoochee R.
Flint R.
GRAND GULF
NATCHEZ
Tombigbee R.
ALEXANDRIA
Sabine R.
PORT HUDSON
BATON ROUGE
MOBILE
PENSACOLA
FLO
O.
TALLAHASSE
Apalachicola R.
NEW ORLEANS
Mobile Bay
FT MORGAN
FT PICKENS
FT JACKSON
FT ST PHILIP

GULF OF MEXICO